C-3719   CAREER EXAMINATION SERIES

This is your
PASSBOOK for...

Forensic Program Aide

Test Preparation Study Guide
Questions & Answers

COPYRIGHT NOTICE

This book is SOLELY intended for, is sold ONLY to, and its use is RESTRICTED to individual, bona fide applicants or candidates who qualify by virtue of having seriously filed applications for appropriate license, certificate, professional and/or promotional advancement, higher school matriculation, scholarship, or other legitimate requirements of education and/or governmental authorities.

This book is NOT intended for use, class instruction, tutoring, training, duplication, copying, reprinting, excerption, or adaptation, etc., by:

1) Other publishers
2) Proprietors and/or Instructors of "Coaching" and/or Preparatory Courses
3) Personnel and/or Training Divisions of commercial, industrial, and governmental organizations
4) Schools, colleges, or universities and/or their departments and staffs, including teachers and other personnel
5) Testing Agencies or Bureaus
6) Study groups which seek by the purchase of a single volume to copy and/or duplicate and/or adapt this material for use by the group as a whole without having purchased individual volumes for each of the members of the group
7) Et al.

Such persons would be in violation of appropriate Federal and State statutes.

PROVISION OF LICENSING AGREEMENTS – Recognized educational, commercial, industrial, and governmental institutions and organizations, and others legitimately engaged in educational pursuits, including training, testing, and measurement activities, may address request for a licensing agreement to the copyright owners, who will determine whether, and under what conditions, including fees and charges, the materials in this book may be used them. In other words, a licensing facility exists for the legitimate use of the material in this book on other than an individual basis. However, it is asseverated and affirmed here that the material in this book CANNOT be used without the receipt of the express permission of such a licensing agreement from the Publishers. Inquiries re licensing should be addressed to the company, attention rights and permissions department.

All rights reserved, including the right of reproduction in whole or in part, in any form or by any means, electronic or mechanical, including photocopying, recording, or by any information storage and retrieval system, without permission in writing from the Publisher.

Copyright © 2025 by
National Learning Corporation

212 Michael Drive, Syosset, NY 11791
(516) 921-8888 • www.passbooks.com
E-mail: info@passbooks.com

PASSBOOK® SERIES

THE *PASSBOOK® SERIES* has been created to prepare applicants and candidates for the ultimate academic battlefield – the examination room.

At some time in our lives, each and every one of us may be required to take an examination – for validation, matriculation, admission, qualification, registration, certification, or licensure.

Based on the assumption that every applicant or candidate has met the basic formal educational standards, has taken the required number of courses, and read the necessary texts, the *PASSBOOK® SERIES* furnishes the one special preparation which may assure passing with confidence, instead of failing with insecurity. Examination questions – together with answers – are furnished as the basic vehicle for study so that the mysteries of the examination and its compounding difficulties may be eliminated or diminished by a sure method.

This book is meant to help you pass your examination provided that you qualify and are serious in your objective.

The entire field is reviewed through the huge store of content information which is succinctly presented through a provocative and challenging approach – the question-and-answer method.

A climate of success is established by furnishing the correct answers at the end of each test.

You soon learn to recognize types of questions, forms of questions, and patterns of questioning. You may even begin to anticipate expected outcomes.

You perceive that many questions are repeated or adapted so that you can gain acute insights, which may enable you to score many sure points.

You learn how to confront new questions, or types of questions, and to attack them confidently and work out the correct answers.

You note objectives and emphases, and recognize pitfalls and dangers, so that you may make positive educational adjustments.

Moreover, you are kept fully informed in relation to new concepts, methods, practices, and directions in the field.

You discover that you are actually taking the examination all the time: you are preparing for the examination by "taking" an examination, not by reading extraneous and/or supererogatory textbooks.

In short, this PASSBOOK®, used directedly, should be an important factor in helping you to pass your test.

FORENSIC PROGRAM AIDE

DUTIES
As a Forensic Program Aide, you would provide treatment and a safe, therapeutic physical and interpersonal environment for mentally ill patients, most of whom are defendants in a criminal proceeding.

SUBJECT OF EXAMINATIONS
The written test will be designed to test for knowledge, skills, and/or abilities in such areas as:
1. First aid and basic patient care;
2. Characteristics of patient population; and
3. Treatment for patient population.

HOW TO TAKE A TEST

I. YOU MUST PASS AN EXAMINATION

A. *WHAT EVERY CANDIDATE SHOULD KNOW*

Examination applicants often ask us for help in preparing for the written test. What can I study in advance? What kinds of questions will be asked? How will the test be given? How will the papers be graded?

As an applicant for a civil service examination, you may be wondering about some of these things. Our purpose here is to suggest effective methods of advance study and to describe civil service examinations.

Your chances for success on this examination can be increased if you know how to prepare. Those "pre-examination jitters" can be reduced if you know what to expect. You can even experience an adventure in good citizenship if you know why civil service exams are given.

B. *WHY ARE CIVIL SERVICE EXAMINATIONS GIVEN?*

Civil service examinations are important to you in two ways. As a citizen, you want public jobs filled by employees who know how to do their work. As a job seeker, you want a fair chance to compete for that job on an equal footing with other candidates. The best-known means of accomplishing this two-fold goal is the competitive examination.

Exams are widely publicized throughout the nation. They may be administered for jobs in federal, state, city, municipal, town or village governments or agencies.

Any citizen may apply, with some limitations, such as the age or residence of applicants. Your experience and education may be reviewed to see whether you meet the requirements for the particular examination. When these requirements exist, they are reasonable and applied consistently to all applicants. Thus, a competitive examination may cause you some uneasiness now, but it is your privilege and safeguard.

C. *HOW ARE CIVIL SERVICE EXAMS DEVELOPED?*

Examinations are carefully written by trained technicians who are specialists in the field known as "psychological measurement," in consultation with recognized authorities in the field of work that the test will cover. These experts recommend the subject matter areas or skills to be tested; only those knowledges or skills important to your success on the job are included. The most reliable books and source materials available are used as references. Together, the experts and technicians judge the difficulty level of the questions.

Test technicians know how to phrase questions so that the problem is clearly stated. Their ethics do not permit "trick" or "catch" questions. Questions may have been tried out on sample groups, or subjected to statistical analysis, to determine their usefulness.

Written tests are often used in combination with performance tests, ratings of training and experience, and oral interviews. All of these measures combine to form the best-known means of finding the right person for the right job.

II. HOW TO PASS THE WRITTEN TEST

A. NATURE OF THE EXAMINATION

To prepare intelligently for civil service examinations, you should know how they differ from school examinations you have taken. In school you were assigned certain definite pages to read or subjects to cover. The examination questions were quite detailed and usually emphasized memory. Civil service exams, on the other hand, try to discover your present ability to perform the duties of a position, plus your potentiality to learn these duties. In other words, a civil service exam attempts to predict how successful you will be. Questions cover such a broad area that they cannot be as minute and detailed as school exam questions.

In the public service similar kinds of work, or positions, are grouped together in one "class." This process is known as *position-classification*. All the positions in a class are paid according to the salary range for that class. One class title covers all of these positions, and they are all tested by the same examination.

B. FOUR BASIC STEPS

1) Study the announcement

How, then, can you know what subjects to study? Our best answer is: "Learn as much as possible about the class of positions for which you've applied." The exam will test the knowledge, skills and abilities needed to do the work.

Your most valuable source of information about the position you want is the official exam announcement. This announcement lists the training and experience qualifications. Check these standards and apply only if you come reasonably close to meeting them.

The brief description of the position in the examination announcement offers some clues to the subjects which will be tested. Think about the job itself. Review the duties in your mind. Can you perform them, or are there some in which you are rusty? Fill in the blank spots in your preparation.

Many jurisdictions preview the written test in the exam announcement by including a section called "Knowledge and Abilities Required," "Scope of the Examination," or some similar heading. Here you will find out specifically what fields will be tested.

2) Review your own background

Once you learn in general what the position is all about, and what you need to know to do the work, ask yourself which subjects you already know fairly well and which need improvement. You may wonder whether to concentrate on improving your strong areas or on building some background in your fields of weakness. When the announcement has specified "some knowledge" or "considerable knowledge," or has used adjectives like "beginning principles of..." or "advanced ... methods," you can get a clue as to the number and difficulty of questions to be asked in any given field. More questions, and hence broader coverage, would be included for those subjects which are more important in the work. Now weigh your strengths and weaknesses against the job requirements and prepare accordingly.

3) Determine the level of the position

Another way to tell how intensively you should prepare is to understand the level of the job for which you are applying. Is it the entering level? In other words, is this the position in which beginners in a field of work are hired? Or is it an intermediate or advanced level? Sometimes this is indicated by such words as "Junior" or "Senior" in the class title. Other jurisdictions use Roman numerals to designate the level – Clerk I, Clerk II, for example. The word "Supervisor" sometimes appears in the title. If the level is not indicated by the title, check the description of duties. Will you be working under very close supervision, or will you have responsibility for independent decisions in this work?

4) Choose appropriate study materials

Now that you know the subjects to be examined and the relative amount of each subject to be covered, you can choose suitable study materials. For beginning level jobs, or even advanced ones, if you have a pronounced weakness in some aspect of your training, read a modern, standard textbook in that field. Be sure it is up to date and has general coverage. Such books are normally available at your library, and the librarian will be glad to help you locate one. For entry-level positions, questions of appropriate difficulty are chosen – neither highly advanced questions, nor those too simple. Such questions require careful thought but not advanced training.

If the position for which you are applying is technical or advanced, you will read more advanced, specialized material. If you are already familiar with the basic principles of your field, elementary textbooks would waste your time. Concentrate on advanced textbooks and technical periodicals. Think through the concepts and review difficult problems in your field.

These are all general sources. You can get more ideas on your own initiative, following these leads. For example, training manuals and publications of the government agency which employs workers in your field can be useful, particularly for technical and professional positions. A letter or visit to the government department involved may result in more specific study suggestions, and certainly will provide you with a more definite idea of the exact nature of the position you are seeking.

III. KINDS OF TESTS

Tests are used for purposes other than measuring knowledge and ability to perform specified duties. For some positions, it is equally important to test ability to make adjustments to new situations or to profit from training. In others, basic mental abilities not dependent on information are essential. Questions which test these things may not appear as pertinent to the duties of the position as those which test for knowledge and information. Yet they are often highly important parts of a fair examination. For very general questions, it is almost impossible to help you direct your study efforts. What we can do is to point out some of the more common of these general abilities needed in public service positions and describe some typical questions.

1) General information

Broad, general information has been found useful for predicting job success in some kinds of work. This is tested in a variety of ways, from vocabulary lists to questions about current events. Basic background in some field of work, such as sociology or economics, may be sampled in a group of questions. Often these are principles which have become familiar to most persons through exposure rather than through formal training. It is difficult to advise you how to study for these questions; being alert to the world around you is our best suggestion.

2) Verbal ability

An example of an ability needed in many positions is verbal or language ability. Verbal ability is, in brief, the ability to use and understand words. Vocabulary and grammar tests are typical measures of this ability. Reading comprehension or paragraph interpretation questions are common in many kinds of civil service tests. You are given a paragraph of written material and asked to find its central meaning.

3) Numerical ability

Number skills can be tested by the familiar arithmetic problem, by checking paired lists of numbers to see which are alike and which are different, or by interpreting charts and graphs. In the latter test, a graph may be printed in the test booklet which you are asked to use as the basis for answering questions.

4) Observation

A popular test for law-enforcement positions is the observation test. A picture is shown to you for several minutes, then taken away. Questions about the picture test your ability to observe both details and larger elements.

5) Following directions

In many positions in the public service, the employee must be able to carry out written instructions dependably and accurately. You may be given a chart with several columns, each column listing a variety of information. The questions require you to carry out directions involving the information given in the chart.

6) Skills and aptitudes

Performance tests effectively measure some manual skills and aptitudes. When the skill is one in which you are trained, such as typing or shorthand, you can practice. These tests are often very much like those given in business school or high school courses. For many of the other skills and aptitudes, however, no short-time preparation can be made. Skills and abilities natural to you or that you have developed throughout your lifetime are being tested.

Many of the general questions just described provide all the data needed to answer the questions and ask you to use your reasoning ability to find the answers. Your best preparation for these tests, as well as for tests of facts and ideas, is to be at your physical and mental best. You, no doubt, have your own methods of getting into an exam-taking mood and keeping "in shape." The next section lists some ideas on this subject.

IV. KINDS OF QUESTIONS

Only rarely is the "essay" question, which you answer in narrative form, used in civil service tests. Civil service tests are usually of the short-answer type. Full instructions for answering these questions will be given to you at the examination. But in case this is your first experience with short-answer questions and separate answer sheets, here is what you need to know:

1) Multiple-choice Questions

Most popular of the short-answer questions is the "multiple choice" or "best answer" question. It can be used, for example, to test for factual knowledge, ability to solve problems or judgment in meeting situations found at work.

A multiple-choice question is normally one of three types—
- It can begin with an incomplete statement followed by several possible endings. You are to find the one ending which *best* completes the statement, although some of the others may not be entirely wrong.
- It can also be a complete statement in the form of a question which is answered by choosing one of the statements listed.

- It can be in the form of a problem – again you select the best answer.

Here is an example of a multiple-choice question with a discussion which should give you some clues as to the method for choosing the right answer:

When an employee has a complaint about his assignment, the action which will *best* help him overcome his difficulty is to
- A. discuss his difficulty with his coworkers
- B. take the problem to the head of the organization
- C. take the problem to the person who gave him the assignment
- D. say nothing to anyone about his complaint

In answering this question, you should study each of the choices to find which is best. Consider choice "A" – Certainly an employee may discuss his complaint with fellow employees, but no change or improvement can result, and the complaint remains unresolved. Choice "B" is a poor choice since the head of the organization probably does not know what assignment you have been given, and taking your problem to him is known as "going over the head" of the supervisor. The supervisor, or person who made the assignment, is the person who can clarify it or correct any injustice. Choice "C" is, therefore, correct. To say nothing, as in choice "D," is unwise. Supervisors have and interest in knowing the problems employees are facing, and the employee is seeking a solution to his problem.

2) True/False Questions

The "true/false" or "right/wrong" form of question is sometimes used. Here a complete statement is given. Your job is to decide whether the statement is right or wrong.

SAMPLE: A roaming cell-phone call to a nearby city costs less than a non-roaming call to a distant city.

This statement is wrong, or false, since roaming calls are more expensive.

This is not a complete list of all possible question forms, although most of the others are variations of these common types. You will always get complete directions for answering questions. Be sure you understand *how* to mark your answers – ask questions until you do.

V. RECORDING YOUR ANSWERS

Computer terminals are used more and more today for many different kinds of exams.

For an examination with very few applicants, you may be told to record your answers in the test booklet itself. Separate answer sheets are much more common. If this separate answer sheet is to be scored by machine – and this is often the case – it is highly important that you mark your answers correctly in order to get credit.

An electronic scoring machine is often used in civil service offices because of the speed with which papers can be scored. Machine-scored answer sheets must be marked with a pencil, which will be given to you. This pencil has a high graphite content which responds to the electronic scoring machine. As a matter of fact, stray dots may register as answers, so do not let your pencil rest on the answer sheet while you are pondering the correct answer. Also, if your pencil lead breaks or is otherwise defective, ask for another.

Since the answer sheet will be dropped in a slot in the scoring machine, be careful not to bend the corners or get the paper crumpled.

The answer sheet normally has five vertical columns of numbers, with 30 numbers to a column. These numbers correspond to the question numbers in your test booklet. After each number, going across the page are four or five pairs of dotted lines. These short dotted lines have small letters or numbers above them. The first two pairs may also have a "T" or "F" above the letters. This indicates that the first two pairs only are to be used if the questions are of the true-false type. If the questions are multiple choice, disregard the "T" and "F" and pay attention only to the small letters or numbers.

Answer your questions in the manner of the sample that follows:

32. The largest city in the United States is
    A. Washington, D.C.
    B. New York City
    C. Chicago
    D. Detroit
    E. San Francisco

1) Choose the answer you think is best. (New York City is the largest, so "B" is correct.)
2) Find the row of dotted lines numbered the same as the question you are answering. (Find row number 32)
3) Find the pair of dotted lines corresponding to the answer. (Find the pair of lines under the mark "B.")
4) Make a solid black mark between the dotted lines.

VI. BEFORE THE TEST

Common sense will help you find procedures to follow to get ready for an examination. Too many of us, however, overlook these sensible measures. Indeed, nervousness and fatigue have been found to be the most serious reasons why applicants fail to do their best on civil service tests. Here is a list of reminders:

- Begin your preparation early – Don't wait until the last minute to go scurrying around for books and materials or to find out what the position is all about.
- Prepare continuously – An hour a night for a week is better than an all-night cram session. This has been definitely established. What is more, a night a week for a month will return better dividends than crowding your study into a shorter period of time.
- Locate the place of the exam – You have been sent a notice telling you when and where to report for the examination. If the location is in a different town or otherwise unfamiliar to you, it would be well to inquire the best route and learn something about the building.
- Relax the night before the test – Allow your mind to rest. Do not study at all that night. Plan some mild recreation or diversion; then go to bed early and get a good night's sleep.
- Get up early enough to make a leisurely trip to the place for the test – This way unforeseen events, traffic snarls, unfamiliar buildings, etc. will not upset you.
- Dress comfortably – A written test is not a fashion show. You will be known by number and not by name, so wear something comfortable.

- Leave excess paraphernalia at home – Shopping bags and odd bundles will get in your way. You need bring only the items mentioned in the official notice you received; usually everything you need is provided. Do not bring reference books to the exam. They will only confuse those last minutes and be taken away from you when in the test room.
- Arrive somewhat ahead of time – If because of transportation schedules you must get there very early, bring a newspaper or magazine to take your mind off yourself while waiting.
- Locate the examination room – When you have found the proper room, you will be directed to the seat or part of the room where you will sit. Sometimes you are given a sheet of instructions to read while you are waiting. Do not fill out any forms until you are told to do so; just read them and be prepared.
- Relax and prepare to listen to the instructions
- If you have any physical problem that may keep you from doing your best, be sure to tell the test administrator. If you are sick or in poor health, you really cannot do your best on the exam. You can come back and take the test some other time.

VII. AT THE TEST

The day of the test is here and you have the test booklet in your hand. The temptation to get going is very strong. Caution! There is more to success than knowing the right answers. You must know how to identify your papers and understand variations in the type of short-answer question used in this particular examination. Follow these suggestions for maximum results from your efforts:

1) Cooperate with the monitor

The test administrator has a duty to create a situation in which you can be as much at ease as possible. He will give instructions, tell you when to begin, check to see that you are marking your answer sheet correctly, and so on. He is not there to guard you, although he will see that your competitors do not take unfair advantage. He wants to help you do your best.

2) Listen to all instructions

Don't jump the gun! Wait until you understand all directions. In most civil service tests you get more time than you need to answer the questions. So don't be in a hurry. Read each word of instructions until you clearly understand the meaning. Study the examples, listen to all announcements and follow directions. Ask questions if you do not understand what to do.

3) Identify your papers

Civil service exams are usually identified by number only. You will be assigned a number; you must not put your name on your test papers. Be sure to copy your number correctly. Since more than one exam may be given, copy your exact examination title.

4) Plan your time

Unless you are told that a test is a "speed" or "rate of work" test, speed itself is usually not important. Time enough to answer all the questions will be provided, but this does not mean that you have all day. An overall time limit has been set. Divide the total time (in minutes) by the number of questions to determine the approximate time you have for each question.

5) Do not linger over difficult questions

If you come across a difficult question, mark it with a paper clip (useful to have along) and come back to it when you have been through the booklet. One caution if you do this – be sure to skip a number on your answer sheet as well. Check often to be sure that you have not lost your place and that you are marking in the row numbered the same as the question you are answering.

6) Read the questions

Be sure you know what the question asks! Many capable people are unsuccessful because they failed to *read* the questions correctly.

7) Answer all questions

Unless you have been instructed that a penalty will be deducted for incorrect answers, it is better to guess than to omit a question.

8) Speed tests

It is often better NOT to guess on speed tests. It has been found that on timed tests people are tempted to spend the last few seconds before time is called in marking answers at random – without even reading them – in the hope of picking up a few extra points. To discourage this practice, the instructions may warn you that your score will be "corrected" for guessing. That is, a penalty will be applied. The incorrect answers will be deducted from the correct ones, or some other penalty formula will be used.

9) Review your answers

If you finish before time is called, go back to the questions you guessed or omitted to give them further thought. Review other answers if you have time.

10) Return your test materials

If you are ready to leave before others have finished or time is called, take ALL your materials to the monitor and leave quietly. Never take any test material with you. The monitor can discover whose papers are not complete, and taking a test booklet may be grounds for disqualification.

VIII. EXAMINATION TECHNIQUES

1) Read the general instructions carefully. These are usually printed on the first page of the exam booklet. As a rule, these instructions refer to the timing of the examination; the fact that you should not start work until the signal and must stop work at a signal, etc. If there are any *special* instructions, such as a choice of questions to be answered, make sure that you note this instruction carefully.

2) When you are ready to start work on the examination, that is as soon as the signal has been given, read the instructions to each question booklet, underline any key words or phrases, such as *least, best, outline, describe* and the like. In this way you will tend to answer as requested rather than discover on reviewing your paper that you *listed without describing*, that you selected the *worst* choice rather than the *best* choice, etc.

3) If the examination is of the objective or multiple-choice type – that is, each question will also give a series of possible answers: A, B, C or D, and you are called upon to select the best answer and write the letter next to that answer on your answer paper – it is advisable to start answering each question in turn. There may be anywhere from 50 to 100 such questions in the three or four hours allotted and you can see how much time would be taken if you read through all the questions before beginning to answer any. Furthermore, if you come across a question or group of questions which you know would be difficult to answer, it would undoubtedly affect your handling of all the other questions.

4) If the examination is of the essay type and contains but a few questions, it is a moot point as to whether you should read all the questions before starting to answer any one. Of course, if you are given a choice – say five out of seven and the like – then it is essential to read all the questions so you can eliminate the two that are most difficult. If, however, you are asked to answer all the questions, there may be danger in trying to answer the easiest one first because you may find that you will spend too much time on it. The best technique is to answer the first question, then proceed to the second, etc.

5) Time your answers. Before the exam begins, write down the time it started, then add the time allowed for the examination and write down the time it must be completed, then divide the time available somewhat as follows:
   - If 3-1/2 hours are allowed, that would be 210 minutes. If you have 80 objective-type questions, that would be an average of 2-1/2 minutes per question. Allow yourself no more than 2 minutes per question, or a total of 160 minutes, which will permit about 50 minutes to review.
   - If for the time allotment of 210 minutes there are 7 essay questions to answer, that would average about 30 minutes a question. Give yourself only 25 minutes per question so that you have about 35 minutes to review.

6) The most important instruction is to *read each question* and make sure you know what is wanted. The second most important instruction is to *time yourself properly* so that you answer every question. The third most important instruction is to *answer every question*. Guess if you have to but include something for each question. Remember that you will receive no credit for a blank and will probably receive some credit if you write something in answer to an essay question. If you guess a letter – say "B" for a multiple-choice question – you may have guessed right. If you leave a blank as an answer to a multiple-choice question, the examiners may respect your feelings but it will not add a point to your score. Some exams may penalize you for wrong answers, so in such cases *only*, you may not want to guess unless you have some basis for your answer.

7) Suggestions
   a. Objective-type questions
      1. Examine the question booklet for proper sequence of pages and questions
      2. Read all instructions carefully
      3. Skip any question which seems too difficult; return to it after all other questions have been answered
      4. Apportion your time properly; do not spend too much time on any single question or group of questions

5. Note and underline key words – *all, most, fewest, least, best, worst, same, opposite,* etc.
6. Pay particular attention to negatives
7. Note unusual option, e.g., unduly long, short, complex, different or similar in content to the body of the question
8. Observe the use of "hedging" words – *probably, may, most likely,* etc.
9. Make sure that your answer is put next to the same number as the question
10. Do not second-guess unless you have good reason to believe the second answer is definitely more correct
11. Cross out original answer if you decide another answer is more accurate; do not erase until you are ready to hand your paper in
12. Answer all questions; guess unless instructed otherwise
13. Leave time for review

  b. Essay questions
1. Read each question carefully
2. Determine exactly what is wanted. Underline key words or phrases.
3. Decide on outline or paragraph answer
4. Include many different points and elements unless asked to develop any one or two points or elements
5. Show impartiality by giving pros and cons unless directed to select one side only
6. Make and write down any assumptions you find necessary to answer the questions
7. Watch your English, grammar, punctuation and choice of words
8. Time your answers; don't crowd material

8) Answering the essay question

Most essay questions can be answered by framing the specific response around several key words or ideas. Here are a few such key words or ideas:

M's: manpower, materials, methods, money, management
P's: purpose, program, policy, plan, procedure, practice, problems, pitfalls, personnel, public relations

  a. Six basic steps in handling problems:
1. Preliminary plan and background development
2. Collect information, data and facts
3. Analyze and interpret information, data and facts
4. Analyze and develop solutions as well as make recommendations
5. Prepare report and sell recommendations
6. Install recommendations and follow up effectiveness

  b. Pitfalls to avoid
1. *Taking things for granted* – A statement of the situation does not necessarily imply that each of the elements is necessarily true; for example, a complaint may be invalid and biased so that all that can be taken for granted is that a complaint has been registered

2. *Considering only one side of a situation* – Wherever possible, indicate several alternatives and then point out the reasons you selected the best one
3. *Failing to indicate follow up* – Whenever your answer indicates action on your part, make certain that you will take proper follow-up action to see how successful your recommendations, procedures or actions turn out to be
4. *Taking too long in answering any single question* – Remember to time your answers properly

IX. AFTER THE TEST

Scoring procedures differ in detail among civil service jurisdictions although the general principles are the same. Whether the papers are hand-scored or graded by machine we have described, they are nearly always graded by number. That is, the person who marks the paper knows only the number – never the name – of the applicant. Not until all the papers have been graded will they be matched with names. If other tests, such as training and experience or oral interview ratings have been given, scores will be combined. Different parts of the examination usually have different weights. For example, the written test might count 60 percent of the final grade, and a rating of training and experience 40 percent. In many jurisdictions, veterans will have a certain number of points added to their grades.

After the final grade has been determined, the names are placed in grade order and an eligible list is established. There are various methods for resolving ties between those who get the same final grade – probably the most common is to place first the name of the person whose application was received first. Job offers are made from the eligible list in the order the names appear on it. You will be notified of your grade and your rank as soon as all these computations have been made. This will be done as rapidly as possible.

People who are found to meet the requirements in the announcement are called "eligibles." Their names are put on a list of eligible candidates. An eligible's chances of getting a job depend on how high he stands on this list and how fast agencies are filling jobs from the list.

When a job is to be filled from a list of eligibles, the agency asks for the names of people on the list of eligibles for that job. When the civil service commission receives this request, it sends to the agency the names of the three people highest on this list. Or, if the job to be filled has specialized requirements, the office sends the agency the names of the top three persons who meet these requirements from the general list.

The appointing officer makes a choice from among the three people whose names were sent to him. If the selected person accepts the appointment, the names of the others are put back on the list to be considered for future openings.

That is the rule in hiring from all kinds of eligible lists, whether they are for typist, carpenter, chemist, or something else. For every vacancy, the appointing officer has his choice of any one of the top three eligibles on the list. This explains why the person whose name is on top of the list sometimes does not get an appointment when some of the persons lower on the list do. If the appointing officer chooses the second or third eligible, the No. 1 eligible does not get a job at once, but stays on the list until he is appointed or the list is terminated.

X. HOW TO PASS THE INTERVIEW TEST

The examination for which you applied requires an oral interview test. You have already taken the written test and you are now being called for the interview test – the final part of the formal examination.

You may think that it is not possible to prepare for an interview test and that there are no procedures to follow during an interview. Our purpose is to point out some things you can do in advance that will help you and some good rules to follow and pitfalls to avoid while you are being interviewed.

What is an interview supposed to test?

The written examination is designed to test the technical knowledge and competence of the candidate; the oral is designed to evaluate intangible qualities, not readily measured otherwise, and to establish a list showing the relative fitness of each candidate – as measured against his competitors – for the position sought. Scoring is not on the basis of "right" and "wrong," but on a sliding scale of values ranging from "not passable" to "outstanding." As a matter of fact, it is possible to achieve a relatively low score without a single "incorrect" answer because of evident weakness in the qualities being measured.

Occasionally, an examination may consist entirely of an oral test – either an individual or a group oral. In such cases, information is sought concerning the technical knowledges and abilities of the candidate, since there has been no written examination for this purpose. More commonly, however, an oral test is used to supplement a written examination.

Who conducts interviews?

The composition of oral boards varies among different jurisdictions. In nearly all, a representative of the personnel department serves as chairman. One of the members of the board may be a representative of the department in which the candidate would work. In some cases, "outside experts" are used, and, frequently, a businessman or some other representative of the general public is asked to serve. Labor and management or other special groups may be represented. The aim is to secure the services of experts in the appropriate field.

However the board is composed, it is a good idea (and not at all improper or unethical) to ascertain in advance of the interview who the members are and what groups they represent. When you are introduced to them, you will have some idea of their backgrounds and interests, and at least you will not stutter and stammer over their names.

What should be done before the interview?

While knowledge about the board members is useful and takes some of the surprise element out of the interview, there is other preparation which is more substantive. It *is* possible to prepare for an oral interview – in several ways:

1) Keep a copy of your application and review it carefully before the interview

This may be the only document before the oral board, and the starting point of the interview. Know what education and experience you have listed there, and the sequence and dates of all of it. Sometimes the board will ask you to review the highlights of your experience for them; you should not have to hem and haw doing it.

2) Study the class specification and the examination announcement

Usually, the oral board has one or both of these to guide them. The qualities, characteristics or knowledges required by the position sought are stated in these documents. They offer valuable clues as to the nature of the oral interview. For example, if the job involves supervisory responsibilities, the announcement will usually indicate that knowledge of modern supervisory methods and the qualifications of the candidate as a supervisor will be tested. If so, you can expect such questions, frequently in the form of a hypothetical situation which you are expected to solve. NEVER go into an oral without knowledge of the duties and responsibilities of the job you seek.

3) Think through each qualification required

Try to visualize the kind of questions you would ask if you were a board member. How well could you answer them? Try especially to appraise your own knowledge and background in each area, *measured against the job sought*, and identify any areas in which you are weak. Be critical and realistic – do not flatter yourself.

4) Do some general reading in areas in which you feel you may be weak

For example, if the job involves supervision and your past experience has NOT, some general reading in supervisory methods and practices, particularly in the field of human relations, might be useful. Do NOT study agency procedures or detailed manuals. The oral board will be testing your understanding and capacity, not your memory.

5) Get a good night's sleep and watch your general health and mental attitude

You will want a clear head at the interview. Take care of a cold or any other minor ailment, and of course, no hangovers.

What should be done on the day of the interview?

Now comes the day of the interview itself. Give yourself plenty of time to get there. Plan to arrive somewhat ahead of the scheduled time, particularly if your appointment is in the fore part of the day. If a previous candidate fails to appear, the board might be ready for you a bit early. By early afternoon an oral board is almost invariably behind schedule if there are many candidates, and you may have to wait. Take along a book or magazine to read, or your application to review, but leave any extraneous material in the waiting room when you go in for your interview. In any event, relax and compose yourself.

The matter of dress is important. The board is forming impressions about you – from your experience, your manners, your attitude, and your appearance. Give your personal appearance careful attention. Dress your best, but not your flashiest. Choose conservative, appropriate clothing, and be sure it is immaculate. This is a business interview, and your appearance should indicate that you regard it as such. Besides, being well groomed and properly dressed will help boost your confidence.

Sooner or later, someone will call your name and escort you into the interview room. *This is it.* From here on you are on your own. It is too late for any more preparation. But remember, you asked for this opportunity to prove your fitness, and you are here because your request was granted.

What happens when you go in?

The usual sequence of events will be as follows: The clerk (who is often the board stenographer) will introduce you to the chairman of the oral board, who will introduce you to the other members of the board. Acknowledge the introductions before you sit down. Do not be surprised if you find a microphone facing you or a stenotypist sitting by. Oral interviews are usually recorded in the event of an appeal or other review.

Usually the chairman of the board will open the interview by reviewing the highlights of your education and work experience from your application – primarily for the benefit of the other members of the board, as well as to get the material into the record. Do not interrupt or comment unless there is an error or significant misinterpretation; if that is the case, do not hesitate. But do not quibble about insignificant matters. Also, he will usually ask you some question about your education, experience or your present job – partly to get you to start talking and to establish the interviewing "rapport." He may start the actual questioning, or turn it over to one of the other members. Frequently, each member undertakes the questioning on a particular area, one in which he is perhaps most competent, so you can expect each member to participate in the examination. Because time is limited, you may also expect some rather abrupt switches in the direction the questioning takes, so do not be upset by it. Normally, a board member will not pursue a single line of questioning unless he discovers a particular strength or weakness.

After each member has participated, the chairman will usually ask whether any member has any further questions, then will ask you if you have anything you wish to add. Unless you are expecting this question, it may floor you. Worse, it may start you off on an extended, extemporaneous speech. The board is not usually seeking more information. The question is principally to offer you a last opportunity to present further qualifications or to indicate that you have nothing to add. So, if you feel that a significant qualification or characteristic has been overlooked, it is proper to point it out in a sentence or so. Do not compliment the board on the thoroughness of their examination – they have been sketchy, and you know it. If you wish, merely say, "No thank you, I have nothing further to add." This is a point where you can "talk yourself out" of a good impression or fail to present an important bit of information. Remember, *you close the interview yourself*.

The chairman will then say, "That is all, Mr. _____, thank you." Do not be startled; the interview is over, and quicker than you think. Thank him, gather your belongings and take your leave. Save your sigh of relief for the other side of the door.

How to put your best foot forward

Throughout this entire process, you may feel that the board individually and collectively is trying to pierce your defenses, seek out your hidden weaknesses and embarrass and confuse you. Actually, this is not true. They are obliged to make an appraisal of your qualifications for the job you are seeking, and they want to see you in your best light. Remember, they must interview all candidates and a non-cooperative candidate may become a failure in spite of their best efforts to bring out his qualifications. Here are 15 suggestions that will help you:

1) Be natural – Keep your attitude confident, not cocky

If you are not confident that you can do the job, do not expect the board to be. Do not apologize for your weaknesses, try to bring out your strong points. The board is interested in a positive, not negative, presentation. Cockiness will antagonize any board member and make him wonder if you are covering up a weakness by a false show of strength.

2) Get comfortable, but don't lounge or sprawl

Sit erectly but not stiffly. A careless posture may lead the board to conclude that you are careless in other things, or at least that you are not impressed by the importance of the occasion. Either conclusion is natural, even if incorrect. Do not fuss with your clothing, a pencil or an ashtray. Your hands may occasionally be useful to emphasize a point; do not let them become a point of distraction.

3) Do not wisecrack or make small talk

This is a serious situation, and your attitude should show that you consider it as such. Further, the time of the board is limited – they do not want to waste it, and neither should you.

4) Do not exaggerate your experience or abilities

In the first place, from information in the application or other interviews and sources, the board may know more about you than you think. Secondly, you probably will not get away with it. An experienced board is rather adept at spotting such a situation, so do not take the chance.

5) If you know a board member, do not make a point of it, yet do not hide it

Certainly you are not fooling him, and probably not the other members of the board. Do not try to take advantage of your acquaintanceship – it will probably do you little good.

6) Do not dominate the interview

Let the board do that. They will give you the clues – do not assume that you have to do all the talking. Realize that the board has a number of questions to ask you, and do not try to take up all the interview time by showing off your extensive knowledge of the answer to the first one.

7) Be attentive

You only have 20 minutes or so, and you should keep your attention at its sharpest throughout. When a member is addressing a problem or question to you, give him your undivided attention. Address your reply principally to him, but do not exclude the other board members.

8) Do not interrupt

A board member may be stating a problem for you to analyze. He will ask you a question when the time comes. Let him state the problem, and wait for the question.

9) Make sure you understand the question

Do not try to answer until you are sure what the question is. If it is not clear, restate it in your own words or ask the board member to clarify it for you. However, do not haggle about minor elements.

10) Reply promptly but not hastily

A common entry on oral board rating sheets is "candidate responded readily," or "candidate hesitated in replies." Respond as promptly and quickly as you can, but do not jump to a hasty, ill-considered answer.

11) Do not be peremptory in your answers

A brief answer is proper – but do not fire your answer back. That is a losing game from your point of view. The board member can probably ask questions much faster than you can answer them.

12) Do not try to create the answer you think the board member wants

He is interested in what kind of mind you have and how it works – not in playing games. Furthermore, he can usually spot this practice and will actually grade you down on it.

13) Do not switch sides in your reply merely to agree with a board member

Frequently, a member will take a contrary position merely to draw you out and to see if you are willing and able to defend your point of view. Do not start a debate, yet do not surrender a good position. If a position is worth taking, it is worth defending.

14) Do not be afraid to admit an error in judgment if you are shown to be wrong

The board knows that you are forced to reply without any opportunity for careful consideration. Your answer may be demonstrably wrong. If so, admit it and get on with the interview.

15) Do not dwell at length on your present job

The opening question may relate to your present assignment. Answer the question but do not go into an extended discussion. You are being examined for a *new* job, not your present one. As a matter of fact, try to phrase ALL your answers in terms of the job for which you are being examined.

Basis of Rating

Probably you will forget most of these "do's" and "don'ts" when you walk into the oral interview room. Even remembering them all will not ensure you a passing grade. Perhaps you did not have the qualifications in the first place. But remembering them will help you to put your best foot forward, without treading on the toes of the board members.

Rumor and popular opinion to the contrary notwithstanding, an oral board wants you to make the best appearance possible. They know you are under pressure – but they also want to see how you respond to it as a guide to what your reaction would be under the pressures of the job you seek. They will be influenced by the degree of poise you display, the personal traits you show and the manner in which you respond.

ABOUT THIS BOOK

This book contains tests divided into Examination Sections. Go through each test, answering every question in the margin. We have also attached a sample answer sheet at the back of the book that can be removed and used. At the end of each test look at the answer key and check your answers. On the ones you got wrong, look at the right answer choice and learn. Do not fill in the answers first. Do not memorize the questions and answers, but understand the answer and principles involved. On your test, the questions will likely be different from the samples. Questions are changed and new ones added. If you understand these past questions you should have success with any changes that arise. Tests may consist of several types of questions. We have additional books on each subject should more study be advisable or necessary for you. Finally, the more you study, the better prepared you will be. This book is intended to be the last thing you study before you walk into the examination room. Prior study of relevant texts is also recommended. NLC publishes some of these in our Fundamental Series. Knowledge and good sense are important factors in passing your exam. Good luck also helps. So now study this Passbook, absorb the material contained within and take that knowledge into the examination. Then do your best to pass that exam.

EXAMINATION SECTION

EXAMINATION SECTION
TEST 1

DIRECTIONS: Each question or incomplete statement is followed by several suggested answers or completions. Select the one that BEST answers the question or completes the statement. *PRINT THE LETTER OF THE CORRECT ANSWER IN THE SPACE AT THE RIGHT.*

1. In reporting on a person who thinks he sees objects which are NOT present and may NOT be real, the assistant should describe such an individual as having

    A. claustrophobia B. delusions
    C. hallucinations D. paranoia

    1._____

2. An adolescent who is habitually discontented could BEST be described as

    A. invidious B. plaintive
    C. quibbling D. captious

    2._____

3. Occupational therapy is MOST closely associated with

    A. vocational guidance B. position classification
    C. curative handicraft D. diathermic treatment

    3._____

4. Of the following degrees of deviation from normal mentality, the one indicating the LEAST intelligence is the

    A. moron B. imbecile C. idiot D. borderline

    4._____

5. The person whose duty it is to manage the estate of a minor or of an incompetent is called the

    A. executor B. probate officer
    C. amicus curiae D. guardian

    5._____

6. "Ostensibly a sane person, yet severely mentally ill and dangerous to himself and others," is a description MOST commonly applied to a

    A. psychopath B. paraplegic C. paretic D. paranoid

    6._____

7. The impact upon society of mental disease is MOST adequately indicated by

    A. its responsibility for sex crimes and delinquency
    B. the phenomenal growth of feeble-mindedness in the United States
    C. the increasing number of deaths resulting from it
    D. the burden of its disabling effects on the community

    7._____

8. A deficiency disease is a disorder caused by a(n)

    A. deficiency of medical aid
    B. diet lacking certain vitamins or minerals
    C. lack of proper rest and relaxation
    D. insufficient quantity of sugar in the diet

    8._____

9. Delinquency on the part of a child is believed to result PRIMARILY from

   A. emotional and personality maladjustments
   B. environmental handicaps
   C. physical disability
   D. sociological factors

10. Current interst in child guidance clinics was developed because of an increasing belief that

   A. at least one-tenth of the nation's youth is destined to end in prison if not given systematic guidance
   B. children should be treated as miniature adults
   C. many of the emotional and mental disabilities of later life result from unfortunate childhood experiences
   D. the best interests of the nation require standardization of each child's education

11. *"The fundamental desires for food, shelter, family and approval, and their accompanying instinctive forms of behavior, are among the most important forces in human life because they are essential to and directly connected with the preservation and the welfare of the individual as well as of the race."*
    According to this statement

   A. as long as human beings are permitted to act instinctively they will act wisely
   B. the instinct for self-preservation makes the individual consider his own welfare rather than that of others
   C. racial and individual welfare depend upon the fundamental desires
   D. the preservation of the race demands that instinctive behavior be modified

12. *"The growth of our cities, the increasing tendency to move from one part of the country to another, the existence of people of different cultures in the neighborhood, have together made it more and more difficult to secure group recreation as part of informal family and neighborhood life."*
    According to this statement,

   A. the breaking up of family and neighborhood ties discourages new family and neighborhood group recreation
   B. neighborhood recreation no longer forms a significant part of the larger community
   C. the growth of cities crowds out the development of all recreational activities
   D. the non-English speaking people do not accept new activities easily

13. *"Sublimation consists in directing some inner urge, arising from a lower psychological level, into some channel of interest on a higher psychological level. Pugnaciousness, for example, is directed into some athletic activity involving combat, such as football or boxing, where rules of fair play and the ethics of the game lift the destructive urge for combat into a constructive experience and offer opportunities for the development of character and personality."*
    According to this statement,

   A. the manner of self-expression may be directed into constructive activities
   B. athletic activities such as football and boxing are destructive of character

C. all conscious behavior on high psychological levels indicates the process of sublimation
D. the rules of fair play are inconsistent with pugnaciousness

14. The one of the following statements which can MOST conceivably be characterized as true is:

    A. Generally speaking, the younger a person is, the less easily he can be influenced by suggestion.
    B. If a therapy assistant has sufficient technical knowledge of his duties, it is not necessary for him to exercise tact in dealing with patients.
    C. A therapy assistant should reject entirely hearsay evidence in making a social diagnosis of a case.
    D. One of the characteristics of adolescence is a feeling in the child that he is misunderstood.

15. The statement that those parental attitudes are good which offer emotional security to the child BEST expresses the notion that

    A. emotionally secure children do not have feelings of aggression
    B. children should not be held accountable for their actions
    C. parental attitudes are inadequate which do not give the child feelings of belonging and freedom for experience
    D. a family in which there is economic dependence cannot be good for the child

16. When advised of the need for medical treatment over an extended period of time in a locality some distance from home, the parent of a child with a cardiac ailment decide to send him to a home in another town. The BEST home for the child in this town would be one

    A. in which there are already residing two foster children who require rest and quiet
    B. in which the family is on relief
    C. in which there are two active boys of the same age as this child
    D. with the bathroom and bedroom on the second floor

17. In planning for the vocational rehabilitation of a physically handicapped person, the use of the sheltered workshop can be a very helpful resource.
    Of the following, the client for whom such service would be MOST appropriate is the one who

    A. will need a constructive way to spend his time for an indefinite period
    B. because of advanced age, is unable to compete in the labor market
    C. needs a transitional experience between his medical care and undertaking a regular job
    D. has a handicap which permanently precludes any gainful employment

18. A group counseling service to parents focused on the understanding of child development and parent-child relations is available through

    A. Childville
    B. The Arthur Lehman Counseling Service
    C. The State Association for Mental Health
    D. The Child Study Association of America

19. A patient is being discharged from an institutional setting following an initial diagnosis and stabilizing treatment for a diabetic condition of which he had not been aware. His doctor recommends a diet and medication regime for the patient to follow at home, but the patient is uncertain about his ability to carry this out on his own.
    A community resource that might be MOST helpful in such a situation is a

    A. visiting nurse service
    B. homemaker service
    C. neighborhood health center
    D. dietitian's service

20. "Experience pragmatically suggests that dislocation from cultural roots and customs makes for tension, insecurity, and anxiety. This holds for the child as well as the adolescent, for the new immigrant as well as the second-generation citizen."
    Of the following, the MOST important implication of the above statement is that

    A. anxiety, distress and incapacity are always personal and can be understood best only through an understanding of the child's peresent cultural environment
    B. in order to resolve the conflicts caused by the displacement of a child from a home with one cultural background to one with another, it is essential that the child fully replace his old culture with the new one
    C. no treatment goal can be envisaged for a dislocated child which does not involve a value judgment which is itself culturally determined
    D. anxiety and distress result from a child's reaction to culturally oriented treatment goals

21. Accepting the fact that mentally gifted children represent superior heredity, the United States faces an important eugenic problem CHIEFLY because

    A. unless these mentally gifted children mature and reproduce more rapidly than the less intelligent children, the nation is heading for a lowering of the average intelligence of its people
    B. although the mentally gifted child always excels scholastically, he generally has less physical stamina than the normal child and tends to lower the nation's population physically
    C. the mentally subnormal are increasing more rapidly than the mentally gifted in America, thus affecting the overall level of achievement of the gifted child
    D. unless the mental level of the general population is raised to that of the gifted child, the mentally gifted will eventually usurp the reigns of government and dominate the mentally weaker

22. The form of psychiatric treatment which requires the LEAST amount of participation on the part of the patient is

    A. psychoanalysis   B. psychotherapy
    C. shock therapy   D. non-directive therapy

23. Tests administered by psychologists for the PRIMARY purpose of measuring intelligence are known as _____ tests.

    A. protective   B. validating
    C. psychometric   D. apperception

24. In recent years there have been some significant changes in the treatment of patients in state psychiatric hospitals. These changes are PRIMARILY caused by the use of

    A. electric shock therapy
    B. tranquilizing drugs
    C. steroids
    D. the open ward policy

25. The psychological test which makes use of a set of 20 pictures each depicting a dramatic scene is known as the

    A. Goodenough Test
    B. Thematic Apperception Test
    C. Minnesota Multiphasic Personality Inventory
    D. Healy Picture Completion Test

26. One of the MOST effective ways in which experimental psychologists have been able to study the effects on personality of heredity and environment has been through the study of

    A. primitive cultures
    B. identical twins
    C. mental defectives
    D. newborn infants

27. In hospitals with psychiatric divisions, the psychiatric function is predominantly that of

    A. the training of personnel in all psychiatric disciplines
    B. protection of the community against potentially dangerous psychiatric patients
    C. research and study of psychiatric patients so that new knowledge and information can be made generally available
    D. short-term hospitalization designed to determine diagnosis and recommendations for treatment

28. Predictions of human behavior on the basis of past behavior frequently are inaccurate because

    A. basic patterns of human behavior are in a continual state of flux
    B. human behavior is not susceptible to explanation of a scientific nature
    C. the underlying psychological mechanisms of behavior are not completely understood
    D. quantitative techniques for the measurement of stimuli and responses are unavailable

29. Socio-cultural factors are being re-evaluated in casework practice as they influence both the worker and the client in their participation in the casework process.
Of the following factors, the one which is currently being studied MOST widely is the

    A. social class of worker and client and its significance in casework
    B. difference in native intelligence which can be ascribed to racial origin of an individual
    C. cultural values affecting the areas in which an individual functions
    D. necessity in casework treatment of the client's membership in an organized religious group

30. Deviant behavior is a sociological term used to describe behavior which is not in accord with generally accepted standards. This may include juvenile delinquency, adult criminality, mental or physical illness. Comparison of normal with deviant behavior is useful because it

    A. makes it possible to establish watertight behavioral descriptions
    B. provides evidence of differential social behavior which distinguishes deviant from normal behavior
    C. indicates that deviant behavior is of no concern to caseworkers
    D. provides no evidence that social role is a determinant of behavior

31. Alcoholism may affect an individual client's ability to function as a spouse, parent, worker and citizen. Your responsibility to a client with a history of alcoholism is to

    A. interpret to the client the causes of alcoholism as a disease syndrome
    B. work with the alcoholic's family to accept him as he is and to stop trying to reform him
    C. encourage the family of the alcoholic to accept treatment
    D. determine the origins of his particular drinking problem, establish a diagnosis, and work out a treatment plan for him

32. There is a trend to regard narcotic addiction as a form of illness for which the current methods of intervention have not been effective. Research on the combination of social, psychological and physical causes of addiction would indicate that social workers should

    A. oppose hospitalization of addicts in institutions
    B. encourage the addict to live normally at home
    C. recognize that there is no successful treatment for addiction and act accordingly
    D. use the existing community facilities differentially for each addict

33. A study of social relationships among delinquent and non-delinquent youth has shown that

    A. delinquent youths generally conceal their true feelings and maintain furtive contacts
    B. delinquents are more impulsive and vivacious than law-abiding boys
    C. non-delinquent youths diminish their active social relationships in order to sublimate any anti-social impulses
    D. delinquent and non-delinquent youths exhibit similar characteristics of impulsiveness and vivaciousness

34. The one of the following which is the CHIEF danger of interpreting the delinquent behavior of a child in terms of morality alone when attempting to get at its causes is that

    A. this tends to overlook the likelihood that the causes of the child's actions are more than a negation of morality and involve varied symptoms of disturbance
    B. a child's moral outlook toward life and society is largely colored by that of his parents, thus encouraging parent-child conflicts
    C. too careful a consideration of the moral aspects of the offense and of the child's needs may often negate the demands of justice in a case
    D. standards of morality may be of no concern to the delinquent and he may not realize the seriousness of his offenses

35. An adult with a mental age of 9 years is regarded psychologically as   35.____

    A. of normal mentality   B. a moron
    C. an imbecile   D. an idiot

KEY (CORRECT ANSWERS)

1.	C	16.	A
2.	B	17.	C
3.	C	18.	D
4.	C	19.	A
5.	D	20.	C
6.	A	21.	A
7.	D	22.	C
8.	B	23.	C
9.	A	24.	B
10.	C	25.	B
11.	C	26.	B
12.	A	27.	D
13.	A	28.	C
14.	D	29.	C
15.	C	30.	B

31. D
32. D
33. B
34. A
35. B

EXAMINATION SECTION
TEST 1

DIRECTIONS: Each question or incomplete statement is followed by several suggested answers or completions. Select the one that BEST answers the question or completes the Statement. *PRINT THE LETTER OF THE CORRECT ANSWER IN THE SPACE AT THE RIGHT.*

Questions 1-5.

DIRECTIONS: Answer questions 1 through 5 on the basis of the following passage.

Mental disorders are found in a fairly large number of the inmates in correctional institutions. There are no exact figures as to the inmates who are mentally disturbed -- partly because it is hard to draw a precise line between "mental disturbance" and "normality" -- but 'experts find that somewhere between 15% and 25% of inmates are suffering from disorders that are obvious enough to show up in routine psychiatric examinations. Society has not yet really come to grips with the problem of what to do with mentally disturbed offenders. There is not enough money available to set up treatment programs for all the people identified as mentally disturbed; and there would probably not be enough qualified psychiatric personnel available to run such programs even if they could be set up. Most mentally disturbed offenders are therefore left to serve out their time in correctional institutions, and the burden of dealing with them falls on correction officers. This means that a correction offcer must be sensitive enough to human behavior to know when he is dealing with a person who is not mentally normal, and that the officer must be imaginative enough to be able to sense how an abnormal individual might react under certain circumstances.

1. According to the above passage, mentally disturbed inmakes in correctional institutions

    A. are usually transferred to mental hospitals when their condition is noticed
    B. cannot be told from other inmates, because tests cannot distinguish between insane people and normal people
    C. may constitute as mich as 25% of the total inmate population
    D. should be regarded as no different from all the other inmates

2. The passage says that today the job of handling mentally disturbed inmates is MAINLY up to

    A. psychiatric personnel   B. other inmates
    C. correction officers   D. administrative officials

3. Of the following, which is a reason given in the passage for society's failure to provide adequate treatment programs for mentally disturbed inmates?

    A. Law-abiding citizens should not have to pay for fancy treatment programs for criminals.
    B. A person who breaks the law should not expect society to give him special help.
    C. It is impossible to tell whether an inmate is mentally disturbed.
    D. There are not enough trained people to provide the kind of treatment needed.

4. The expression *abnormal individual,* as used in the last sentence of the passage, refers to an individual who is

   A. of average intelligence
   B. of superior intelligence
   C. completely normal
   D. mentally disturbed

5. The reader of the passage would MOST likely agree that

   A. correction officers should not expect mentally disturbed persons to behave the same way a normal person would behave
   B. correction officers should not report infractions of the rules committed by mentally disturbed persons
   C. mentally disturbed persons who break the law should be treated exactly the same way as anyone else
   D. mentally disturbed persons who have broken the law should not be imprisoned

Questions 6-12.

DIRECTIONS: Questions 6 through 12 are based on the roster of patients, the instructions, the table, and the sample question given below.

Twelve patients of a mental institution are divided into three permanent groups in their workshop. They must be present and accounted for in these groups at the beginning of each workday. During the day, the patients check out of their groups for various activities. They check back in again when those activities have been completed. Assume that the day is divided into three activity periods.

ROSTER OF PATIENTS

GROUP X	Ted	Frank	George	Harry
GROUP Y	Jack	Ken	Larry	Mel
GROUP Z	Phil	Bob	Sam	Vic

The following table shows the movements of these patients from their groups during the day. Assume that all were present and accounted for at the beginning of Period I.

		GROUP X	GROUP Y	GROUP Z
Period I	Check-outs	Ted, Frank	Ken, Larry	Phil
Period II	Check-ins	Frank	Ken, Larry	Phil
	Check-outs	George	Jack, Mel	Bob, Sam, Vic
Period III	Check-ins	George	Mel, Jack	Sam, Bob, Vic
	Check-outs	Frank, Harry	Ken	Vic

SAMPLE QUESTION: At the end of Period II, the patients remaining in Group X were

   A. Ted, Frank, Harry
   B. Frank, Harry
   C. Ted, George
   D. Frank, Harry, George

During Period I, Ted and Frank were checked out from Group X. During Period II, Frank was checked back in and George was checked out. Therefore, the members of the group remaining out are Ted and George. The two other members of the group, Frank and Harry, should be present. The CORRECT answer is B.

6. At the end of Period I, the TOTAL number of patients remaining in their own permanent groups was

   A. 8   B. 7   C. 6   D. 5

7. At the end of Period I, the patients remaining in Group Z were

   A. George and Harry
   B. Jack and Mel
   C. Bob, Sam, and Vic
   D. Phil

8. At the end of Period II, the patients remaining in Group Y were

   A. Ken and Larry
   B. Jack, Ken, and Mel
   C. Jack and Ken
   D. Ken, Mel, and Larry

9. At the end of Period II, the TOTAL number of patients remaining in their own permanent groups was

   A. 8   B. 7   C. 6   D. 5

10. At the end of Period II, the patients who were NOT present in Group Z were

    A. Phil, Bob, and Sam
    B. Sam, Bob, and Vic
    C. Sam, Vic, and Phil
    D. Vic, Phil, and Bob

11. At the end of Period II, the patients remaining in Group Y were

    A. Ted, Frank, and George
    B. Jack, Mel, and Ken
    C. Jack, Larry, and Mel
    D. Frank and Harry

12. At the end of Period III, the TOTAL number of patients NOT present in their own permanent groups was

    A. 4   B. 5   C. 6   D. 7

13. The one of the following conditions which bears no causative relationship to feeblemindedness is

    A. heredity
    B. cerebral defect
    C. early postnatal trauma
    D. dementia

14. Physical conditions which are caused by emotional conflicts are generally referred to as being

    A. psycho-social
    B. hypochondriacal
    C. psychosomatic
    D. psychotic

15. Of the following conditions, the one in which anxiety is NOT generally found is

    A. psychopathic personality
    B. mild hysteria
    C. psychoneurosis
    D. compulsive-obsessive personality

16. Kleptomania may BEST be described as a

    A. neurotic drive to accumulate personal property through compulsive acts in order to dispose of it to others with whom one wishes friendship
    B. type of neurosis which manifests itself in an uncontrollable impulse to steal without economic motivation
    C. psychopathic trait which is probably hereditary in nature
    D. manifestation of punishment-inviting behavior based upon guilt feelings for some other crime or wrong-doing, fantasied or real, committed as a child

17. The one of the following tests which is NOT ordinarily used as a protective technique is the

    A. Wechsler Bellevue Scale
    B. Rorschach Test
    C. Thematic Apperception Test
    D. Jung Free Association Test

18. The outstanding personality test in use at the present time is the Rorschach Test. Of the following considerations, the GREATEST value of this test to the psychiatrist and social worker is that it

    A. provides practical recommendations with reference to further educational and vocational training possibilities for the person tested
    B. reveals in quick, concise form the hereditary factors affecting the individual personality
    C. helps in substantiating a diagnosis of juvenile delinquency
    D. helps in a diagnostic formulation and in determining differential treatment

19. Of the following, the one through which ethical values are MOST generally acquired is

    A. heredity
    B. early training in school
    C. admonition and strict corrective measures by parents and other supervising adults
    D. integration into the self of parental values and attitudes

20. Delinquent behavior is MOST generally a result of

    A. living and growing up in an environment that is both socially and financially deprived
    B. a lack of educational opportunity for development of individual skills
    C. multiple factors -- psychological, bio-social, emotional and environmental
    D. low frustration tolerance of many parents toward problems of married life

21. Alcoholism in the United States is USUALLY caused by

    A. the sense of frustration in one's work
    B. inadequacy of recreational facilities
    C. neurotic conflicts expressed in drinking excessively
    D. shyness and timidity

22. The MOST distinctive characteristic of the chronic alcoholic is that he drinks alcohol 22.____

    A. socially B. compulsively
    C. periodically D. secretly

23. The chronic alcoholic is the person who cannot face reality without alcohol, and yet whose adequate adjustment to reality is impossible so long as he uses alcohol. 23.____
    On the basis of this statement, it is MOST reasonable to conclude that individuals overindulge in alcohol because alcohol

    A. deadens the sense of conflict, giving the individual an illusion of social competence and a feeling of well-being and success
    B. provides the individual with an outlet to display his feelings of good-fellowship and cheerfulness which are characteristic of his extroverted personality
    C. affords an escape technique from habitual irrational fears, but does not affect rational fears
    D. offers an escape from imagery and feelings of superiority which cause tension and anxiety

24. The one of the following drugs to which a person is LEAST likely to become addicted is 24.____

    A. opium B. morphine C. marijuana D. heroin

25. Teenagers who become addicted to the use of drugs are MOST generally 25.____

    A. mentally defective B. paranoid
    C. normally adventurous D. emotionally disturbed

26. In the light of the current high rate of addiction to drugs among youths throughout the country, the one of the following statements which is generally considered to be LEAST correct is that 26.____

    A. a relatively large number of children and youths who experiment with drugs become addicts
    B. youths who use narcotics do so because of some emotional and personality disturbance
    C. youthful addicts are found largely among those who suffer to an abnormal extent deprivations in their personal development and growth
    D. the great majority of youthful addicts have had unfortunate home experiences and practically no contact with established community agencies

27. The one of the following terms which BEST describes the psychological desire to repeat the use of a drug intermittently or continuously because of emotional needs is 27.____

    A. habituation B. euphoria C. tolerance D. addiction

28. The desire for special clothing in a mental institution usually is concerned with 28.____

    A. shoes B. sox C. trousers D. underwear

29. A study entitled "A preliminary evaluation of the relationship between group psychotherapy and the adjustment of adolescent inmates (16-21 years) in a short-term penal institution" was conducted by the Diagnostic Staff at Rikers Island in New York. A conclusion which was drawn as a result of the study was that 29.____

A. a repetition of the study was necessary with smaller therapy and non-therapy groups
B. group psychotherapy subjects displayed a better institutional adjustment than those not receiving group therapy
C. no follow-up study was necessary because of the negative results from the original study
D. a smaller proportion of experimental group subjects improved after receiving group psychotherapy when compared to those who did not receive group therapy

30. The one of the following statements which is MOST accurate concerning group psychotherapy is that group psychotherapy

A. is in a way an outgrowth of the concept of patient self-government
B. is of little value with deviant personality types
C. should make the group members resent help from their fellow patients
D. reflects a punitive rather than a rehabilitative aim

31. In group counseling and psychotherapy it is USUALLY true that persons are more defensive and argumentative than in individualized counseling and therapy sessions. The reason for this tendency is that

A. individuals in a group setting feel it more necessary to protect their personality
B. people in group settings are motivated by the characteristically free atmosphere
C. people would rather argue in a group setting than in an individualized setting
D. the group session is more poorly organized and therefore uncontrolled

32. There is a group of mentally ill patients who have a <u>functional psychosis.</u> The word "functional" in this case indicates that

A. it is an organic psychosis
B. the psychosis is caused by alcoholism or drug addiction
C. there are no demonstrable changes in the brain
D. there are clinical findings of senile arteriosclerosis

33. "Sociopaths" is a fairly new word used to describe

A. confirmed narcotics addicts
B. latent male homosexuals
C. neurotic adolescents
D. psychopathic personalities

34. The incarceration of the geriatric presents many problems in mental administration. The word "geriatric" means MOST NEARLY

A. dipsomanic (alcoholic)
B. moronic (mentally deficient)
C. pertaining to split personality types
D. pertaining to individuals of advanced years

35. Jobs for ex-patients can MOST often be found in

A. big corporations
B. domestic service
C. government agencies
D. small private enterprises

KEY (CORRECT ANSWERS)

1. C
2. C
3. D
4. D
5. A

6. B
7. C
8. A
9. D
10. B

11. C
12. B
13. D
14. C
15. A

16. B
17. A
18. D
19. D
20. C

21. C
22. B
23. A
24. C
25. D

26. A
27. A
28. A
29. B
30. A

31. A
32. C
33. D
34. D
35. D

_____

EXAMINATION SECTION
TEST 1

DIRECTIONS: Each question or incomplete statement is followed by several suggested answers or completions. Select the one that BEST answers the question or completes the statement. *PRINT THE LETTER OF THE CORRECT ANSWER IN THE SPACE AT THE RIGHT.*

1. A relationship in which a patient becomes dependent on the nurse   1._____

    A. is always unprofessional
    B. is inevitably "bad" for the patient
    C. may be necessary temporarily
    D. impedes learning

2. Anxiety is the CHIEF characteristic of the   2._____

    A. immature personality
    B. psychoneurotic disorder
    C. involutional psychotic reaction
    D. mentally retarded adolescent

3. The mode of psychological adjustment known as regression can BEST be described as   3._____

    A. refusing to think of unpleasant situations
    B. changing to a type of behavior which is characteristic of an earlier period in life
    C. reverting to actions characteristic of an historically early or primitive code of behavior
    D. hostility towards persons or objects that prove frustrating

4. The CHIEF danger in the employment of escape mechanisms as a form of adjustment is that they   4._____

    A. do more harm than good
    B. are socially undesirable
    C. make the experience expensive
    D. leave the basic problem unsolved

5. In essential hypertension, there is a(n)   5._____

    A. *increase* in systolic pressure and a *decrease* in diastolic pressure
    B. *decrease* in systolic pressure and an *increase* in diastolic pressure
    C. *increase* in *both* systolic and diastolic pressure
    D. *decrease* in *both* systolic and diastolic pressure

6. The *initial* paralysis in cerebral vascular accident, regardless of cause, is the type known as   6._____

    A. spastic   B. paraplegic   C. flaccid   D. rigid

7. Cerebral hemorrhage *most frequently* occurs in males in the age range from   7._____

    A. 20 to 30 years   B. 30 to 40 years
    C. 40 to 50 years   D. 50 years and over

8. Hereditary progressive muscular dystrophy is a disease characterized by progressive weakness and final atrophy of groups of muscles.
Of the following statements about muscular dystrophy, the one which is LEAST accurate is that

   A. there is no known cure for muscular dystrophy at present
   B. muscular dystrophy is a disease of the central nervous system
   C. early signs of muscular dystrophy are frequent falls, difficulty climbing stairs, development of lordosis, and a waddling gait
   D. therapeutic exercises may have some temporary value in the treatment of muscular dystrophy

9. The home care program is an extension of the hospital's service into the home on an extra-mural basis.
Of the following statements, the one that BEST explains the success of this program is that it

   A. *recognizes* the value to the patient and his family of the preservation of normal family life despite the limitations imposed by the patient's illness
   B. *makes* more hospital beds available for acute illnesses and emergency care
   C. reduces the cost of hospital care by reducing the number of inpatients
   D. *simplifies* hospital administration by reducing the number of chronically ill in hospitals

10. The MOST important of the following reasons for the rehabilitation of the seriously handicapped individual is that

    A. hospitalization of the handicapped is usually prolonged and costly to the community
    B. beds occupied by such patients reduce the number of hospital beds available for acutely ill patients
    C. care of chronically ill or handicapped patients is taxing and difficult for the family, the nurse, and the doctor
    D. it is important to the patient that he be as independent and useful as possible

11. There has been a notable increase in the discharge rate from mental institutions in the state during recent years. This change in statistics may be attributed CHIEFLY to

    A. increasing use of psychoanalysis and better trained personnel
    B. new drugs, changes in admission procedures, and the "open door" policy
    C. the increase in nursing homes for the elderly
    D. the use of psychotherapeutics and early diagnosis of mental illness

12. The PRINCIPAL and BASIC objective of mental hygiene is to

    A. modify attitudes as well as unhealthy behavior secondary to unhealthy attitudes
    B. care for the post-hospitalized psychiatric patient at home
    C. increase mental hygiene clinic services
    D. stimulate interest in improved education for doctors, nurses, and teachers

13. Separation of a child from his own home and placement in a foster home often arouses adverse reactions in the child. Of the following, the one which is MOST serious for the child is   13.____

    A. homesickness
    B. withdrawn behavior
    C. rebellion against authority
    D. dislike of new people

14. Behavior problems of the adolescent school child can BEST be explained by the fact that   14.____

    A. the adolescent suddenly becomes aware of the opposite sex at this time
    B. the demands made on adolescents by intolerant parents create rebellion against authority
    C. during childhood there is a general disregard of the child's need for independence by parents and other adults
    D. adolescence is a transition period between childhood and adulthood which usually creates feelings of insecurity in the adolescent

15. Of the following, the behavior which is LEAST indicative of serious emotional maladjustment in an adolescent boy is   15.____

    A. lying and cheating
    B. shyness and daydreaming
    C. gross overweight
    D. association with a teen-age gang

16. The one of the following diseases which is caused by a birth injury is   16.____

    A. cerebral palsy
    B. meningitis
    C. hydrocele
    D. congenital syphilis
    E. epilepsy

17. A delusion is a   17.____

    A. disharmony of mind and body
    B. fantastic image formed during sleep
    C. false judgment of objective things
    D. cessation of thought
    E. distorted perception or image

18. The one of the following which is the MOST common form of treatment employed by psychiatrists in treating patients with mental disorders is   18.____

    A. hypnotism
    B. hydrotherapy
    C. electroshock
    D. insulin shock
    E. psychotherapy

19. A masochistic person is one who   19.____

    A. is very melancholy
    B. has delusions of grandeur about himself
    C. derives pleasure from being cruelly treated
    D. believes in a fatalistic philosophy
    E. derives pleasure from hurting another

20. Surgery is *ESPECIALLY* difficult during the Oedipal period because of the

    A. father attachment
    B. mental age
    C. castration anxieties
    D. rejection complex
    E. separation from siblings

21. A psychometric test is one which attempts to measure

    A. social adjustment
    B. emotional maturity
    C. physical activity
    D. personality development
    E. Intellectual capacity

22. The one of the following conditions which falls into the classification of a psychosis rather than psychoneurosis is

    A. anxiety hysteria
    B. schizophrenia
    C. neurasthenia
    D. convesion hysteria
    E. compulsion neurosis

23. The one of the following which BEST describes psychosomatic medicine is:

    A. The understanding and treatment of both mind and body in illness
    B. The treatment of disease by psychiatric methods only
    C. The separation of mind and body in medical treatment
    D. The psychological testing of all individuals
    E. A system of socialized medical planning

24. The one of the following conditions for which shock treatment is *FREQUENTLY* used is

    A. alcoholism
    B. Parkinson's syndrome
    C. multiple sclerosis
    D. schizophrenia
    E. diabetes

25. The one of the following conditions which is *NOT* caused by the dysfunction of endocrine glands is

    A. myxedema
    B. duodenal ulcer
    C. cretinism
    D. Addison's disease
    E. none of the above

KEY (CORRECT ANSWERS)

1.	C	11.	B
2.	B	12.	A
3.	B	13.	B
4.	D	14.	D
5.	C	15.	D
6.	C	16.	A
7.	D	17.	C
8.	B	18.	E
9.	A	19.	C
10.	D	20.	C

21. E
22. B
23. A
24. D
25. B

TEST 2

DIRECTIONS: Each question or incomplete statement is followed by several suggested answers or completions. Select the one that BEST answers the question or completes the statement. *PRINT THE LETTER OF THE CORRECT ANSWER IN THE SPACE AT THE RIGHT.*

1. Euphoria is a state of

    A. depression   B. elation   C. ideation   D. frustration

2. An ailment found only in older people is

    A. manic depression   B. dementia praecox
    C. senile dementia   D. tabes dorsalis

3. The permissive policy employed in some mental hospitals is associated with a(n)

    A. increase in assaultive behavior
    B. open door policy
    C. decrease in the use of physical restraint
    D. increase in the use of physical restraint

4. A symptom of dementia praecox is

    A. extroversion   B. tic paralysis
    C. unpredictability   D. cerebral hemorrhage

5. Substituting an activity in which a person can succeed for one in which he may fail is

    A. sublimation   B. projection
    C. rationalization   D. compensation

6. Rationalization is the result of

    A. believing what one wants to believe
    B. reflective thinking
    C. scientific thinking
    D. basing conclusions on fact

7. Delusions of persecution are typical of

    A. epilepsy   B. regression
    C. schizophrenia   D. paranoia

8. A person with an IQ of 85 would be classified as

    A. defective   B. normal
    C. dull average   D. borderline

9. The term describing physical symptoms that do not arise *ENTIRELY* from physical causes is

    A. organic   B. psychoneurotic
    C. psychosomatic   D. psychopathological

10. The mechanism of attributing one's own ideas to others is termed   10.____

    A. projection   B. substitution
    C. sublimation   D. rationalization

11. A child's tendency to pattern after his parents is known as   11.____

    A. identification   B. projection
    C. compensation   D. substitution

12. Stuttering in children *USUALLY* originates from   12.____

    A. physical handicap   B. mentally deficient parents
    C. emotional handicap   D. imitation of other stutterers

13. Acute intoxication may *PROPERLY* be labeled a psychosis because it involves   13.____

    A. intellectual limitations
    B. emotional inadequacies
    C. bodily disease
    D. a severe loss of contact with reality

14. The outstanding change, of the following, in the aging process is that the aged are   14.____

    A. irritable   B. no longer self-reliant
    C. senile   D. easily influenced by stress

15. Re-adjusting the older person to be somewhat self-sufficient is known as   15.____

    A. stabilization   B. regeneration
    C. rejuvenation   D. rehabilitation

16. The spastic child usually   16.____

    A. is mentally retarded   B. is potentially schizophrenic
    C. requires speech training D. has poor vision

17. Insomnia refers to   17.____

    A. unconsciousness   B. sleeplessness
    C. sleep walking   D. insensibility

18. A drug recently introduced in the treatment of mental illness is   18.____

    A. streptomycin   B. paramino-salicylic acid
    C. reserpine   D. cortisone

19. In general, the sleep requirement for an aged person as compared to the sleep requirement for a young adult is   19.____

    A. less   B. more   C. the same   D. slightly greater

20. The *MOST IMPORTANT* aspect of the rehabilitation of a person who has suffered a stroke is the   20.____

    A. patient's emotional reaction to self
    B. doctor's attitude toward the patient
    C. nurse's attitude toward the patient
    D. family reaction toward the patient

21. If a patient tells a nurse that he is contemplating committing suicide, the nurse should

    A. not pay any attention, since people who threaten suicide seldom follow through
    B. urge him to consult a psychiatrist, since potential suicides need psychiatric help immediately
    C. be sympathetic. Her sympathy will divert him from his intention
    D. realize that he is a neurotic with whom she will try to work

22. The BEST advice you can give parents disturbed by their five-year-old child's habit of nailbiting is to tell them to

    A. find out what some of the pressures on the child are and try to relieve them
    B. paint the child's fingers with the product "bitter aloes"
    C. point out to the child that this is a baby habit and not desirable in a school child
    D. punish the child by not allowing him to watch television or go to the movies

23. In certain periods of development, anti-social behavior in young children is considered normal. However, of the following situations, the one which merits referral to a mental hygiene clinic is where

    A. a two-year-old persists in hitting his four-year-old brother
    B. a three-year-old develops enuresis when a new baby is brought into the home
    C. a four-year-old runs away from home at every opportunity
    D. a six-year-old is not friendly, has no "pals" after six months in school, and participates in activities only when compelled to

24. Learning occurs

    A. when the child's responses are adequate
    B. when a solution to the situation is obvious
    C. when the adult solves the problems
    D. None of the above

25. The FIRST emotions to become differentiated may be described as

    A. anger and fear   B. anger and distress
    C. fear and delight   D. delight and distress

KEY (CORRECT ANSWERS)

1.	B	11.	A
2.	C	12.	C
3.	B	13.	D
4.	C	14.	D
5.	D	15.	D
6.	A	16.	C
7.	D	17.	B
8.	C	18.	C
9.	C	19.	A
10.	A	20.	A

21. B
22. A
23. D
24. A
25. D

EXAMINATION SECTION
TEST 1

DIRECTIONS: Each question or incomplete statement is followed by several suggested answers or completions. Select the one that BEST answers the question or completes the statement. *PRINT THE LETTER OF THE CORRECT ANSWER IN THE SPACE AT THE RIGHT.*

1. Marked improvement in a child's ability to draw a man over a brief period of time is MOST likely to be related to 1._____

    A. better social adjustment
    B. maturational effect
    C. the overcoming of a reading disability
    D. recovery from an illness

2. Phenylketonuria, which is associated with intellectual disability, is a disorder of 2._____

    A. the reticuloendothelia system
    B. metabolism
    C. cerebral damage
    D. gyral defect

3. A patient asserts, *I can't stand the agony I suffer when I go against my mother's wishes.* The therapist replies, *You really like to punish that momma inside of you for your dependency, don't you?* 3._____
This response can be viewed as an example of

    A. reassurance   B. interpretation
    C. support   D. reflection of feeling

4. A shy young first grade boy becomes extremely attached to his teacher. He brings her presents, asks her to help him with his clothing a great deal, and wants to sit near her all the time. 4._____
He is MOST likely manifesting the mental mechanism of

    A. introjection   B. sublimation
    C. reaction-formation   D. transference

5. The peculiarities of language behavior in the schizophrenic arise from his extreme need of a feeling of 5._____

    A. personal security   B. self-denial
    C. isolation   D. disarticulation

6. The theory that psychical compensation for a feeling of physical or social inferiority is responsible for the development of a psychoneurosis is attributed to 6._____

    A. Adler   B. Horney   C. Freud   D. Sullivan

7. Which of the following terms refers to the maintenance of stability in the physiological functioning of the organism?

   A. Functional autonomy
   B. Canalization
   C. Homeostasis
   D. Maturation

8. Extensive studies of the personality and behavior of intellectually gifted children generally reveal that they

   A. are physically better developed on the whole than average children
   B. are more likely to be emotionally disturbed than average children
   C. are more prone to divorce in later life than average children
   D. more often come from homes in which emotional disturbance is present

9. Expert opinion of professional workers with the physically handicapped indicates that a list of behavior characteristics would be headed generally by feelings of

   A. aggression   B. hostility   C. inferiority   D. courage

10. Children with pykno-epilepsy suffer from _____ convulsions.

    A. diencephalic
    B. visceral
    C. psychic equivalent
    D. no

11. Children with albinism and aniridia may read MOST comfortably with levels of illumination that, in relation to average levels of illumination, are

    A. upper   B. middle   C. lower   D. uneven

12. Phenylpyruvic amentia has been traced to which of the following?

    A. Nutritional deficiency in the prenatal environment
    B. A single recessive gene
    C. Pathological nidation
    D. Effects of radiation

13. Age of mother has been found to be MOST closely associated with the incidence of which of the following?

    A. Cerebral palsy
    B. Cerebral angiomatosis
    C. Down syndrome
    D. Hydrocephaly

14. The so-called visual area of the cerebral cortex is located in the _____ lobe.

    A. frontal
    B. parietal
    C. occipital
    D. temporal

15. Hypothyroidism is due to _____ in childhood.

    A. thyroid insufficiency
    B. pituitary insufficiency
    C. thyroid excess
    D. pituitary excess

16. The inability to express oneself in words in spite of an adequate understanding and imaginal representation is called

    A. agraphia   B. aphemia   C. agnosia   D. aphexia

17. Clara Thompson saw psychoanalysis as a method of therapy primarily designed to   17.____
    A. give the individual new insights into his past experiences
    B. help the individual master his difficulties in living
    C. have the individual re-enact his relationships with his parents
    D. strengthen the individual's ego defenses

18. According to Freud, the source of the large majority of the dreams recorded during analysis is   18.____
    A. a recent and psychologically significant event which is directly represented in the dream
    B. several recent and significant events which are combined by the dream into a single whole
    C. one or more recent and significant events which are represented in the dream-content by allusion to a contemporary but indifferent event
    D. a subjectively significant experience which is constantly represented in the dream by allusion to a recent but indifferent impression

19. When an individual permits unpleasant impulses or thoughts access to consciousness but does not permit their normal elaboration in associative connections and in affect, the psychoanalytic adjustment mechanism involved is   19.____
    A. rationalization   B. conversion
    C. isolation   D. introjection

20. In psychoanalytic thinking, repression can BEST be thought of as a(n)   20.____
    A. attempt in projection
    B. special type of introjection
    C. reflection of acceptance of Id impulses
    D. temporal form of regression

KEY (CORRECT ANSWERS)

1.	A	11.	C
2.	B	12.	B
3.	B	13.	C
4.	D	14.	C
5.	A	15.	A
6.	A	16.	B
7.	C	17.	B
8.	A	18.	D
9.	C	19.	C
10.	D	20.	D

TEST 2

DIRECTIONS: Each question or incomplete statement is followed by several suggested answers or completions. Select the one that BEST answers the question or completes the statement. *PRINT THE LETTER OF THE CORRECT ANSWER IN THE SPACE AT THE RIGHT.*

1. The behavior pattern considered to be deviate by clinicians is 1.____

    A. infractions of the moral code
    B. generosity
    C. recessive personality
    D. resistance to authority

2. A symptom of dementia praecox is 2.____

    A. tick paralysis
    B. negativism
    C. extroversion
    D. eremophobia

3. According to classic psychoanalytic thinking, the disorder MOST responsive to psycho- 3.____
    analytic therapy is

    A. compulsive neurosis
    B. hysteria
    C. narcissistic neurosis
    D. obsessive neurosis

4. For the therapist, the MOST common meaning of resistance is that it is a(n) 4.____

    A. index of lack of suitability for treatment
    B. defensive attempt on the part of the patient
    C. reflection of superior therapeutic promise
    D. relatively rare phenomenon in psychotherapy

5. In a normal distribution, the percentage of children whose IQ's fall between 90 and 110 is 5.____
    APPROXIMATELY

    A. 40   B. 50   C. 60   D. 70

6. The pioneer in mental diseases who was the first to make a distinction between emo- 6.____
    tional disorder and intellectual disability was

    A. Kraepelin   B. Seguin   C. Esquirol   D. Galton

7. In psychoanalytic thinking, the term superego generally embraces the 7.____

    A. necessary social prohibitions as well as the higher cultural strivings and ideals
    B. unconscious strivings of the person as well as the ego-ideal
    C. unconscious reproaches of the person as well as the id strivings
    D. unconscious ego and its defense mechanism as well as the ego-ideal

8. A major contribution of Fromm to psychoanalysis can be considered to be his 8.____

    A. attempt to formulate the dynamics of orality and the concept of original sin
    B. belief that man has innate social feeling and a drive for perfection
    C. effort to relate the psychological forces operating in man to the society within which he lives
    D. effort to integrate the concept of psychosexual development with Rankian principles

9. José, a ten-year-old, has a hyperthyroid condition. It is MOST likely that his behavior will be characterized by

   A. shyness, withdrawal, and reticence
   B. negativism, aggressiveness, and uncooperativeness
   C. placidity, passivity, and psychomotor delays
   D. restlessness, irritability, and excessive activity

10. The etiology of intellectual disability which is attributed to mechanical damage to the fetus would be classified as

    A. exogenous
    B. endogenous
    C. heterogenous
    D. none of the above

11. The majority of children of intellectually disabled parents will have IQ's that in relation to the IQ's of their parents are

    A. somewhat lower
    B. somewhat higher
    C. lower for boys and higher for girls
    D. lower for girls and higher for boys

12. Stuttering and stammering are MOST likely to develop between the ages of _____ years.

    A. 2 and 5
    B. 6 and 9
    C. 10 and 13
    D. 14 and 18

13. Most cases of stuttering are PRIMARILY the result of

    A. changed handedness
    B. hereditary factors
    C. physiological defects
    D. emotional problems

14. Anorexia is a condition which manifests itself in a loss of

    A. vision
    B. appetite
    C. motor control
    D. smell

15. Most differences in play activities and interests between boys and girls in the elementary school years can PROBABLY be attributed to

    A. inherent biological differences
    B. inherent emotional differences
    C. instinctual influences
    D. cultural influences

16. The rate and pattern of early motor development of children depend MAINLY upon

    A. experience
    B. acculturation
    C. maturation
    D. training

17. Of the following, the BEST index of the anatomical age of young children is

    A. brain weight
    B. ossification
    C. basal metabolism
    D. dentition

18. When children of very superior mental ability are compared in size and weight with children of the same age whose mental ability is average, the former children are found to be

   A. above average
   B. average
   C. below average
   D. either above or below average, depending on the age level

19. The average child speaks his first word at _____ months.

   A. 6   B. 9   C. 12   D. 15

20. In Pavlov's classical study of conditioning, the unconditioned stimulus was the

   A. food
   B. bell
   C. salivation
   D. electric shock

21. Contemporary reinforcement learning theory suggests that the MOST effective learning takes place when correct responses are _____ and incorrect responses _____.

   A. rewarded; ignored
   B. rewarded; punished
   C. ignored; punished
   D. none of the above

22. According to the literature, girls tend to develop physiologically and socially about

   A. the same as boys
   B. one to two years more slowly than boys
   C. one to two years more quickly than boys
   D. none of the above

23. The mother of a newborn infant is told by her physician that she will have to have corrective surgery performed within the next 2 years. It is expected that the operation in addition to her convalescence will keep her away from her baby approximately one month. The period during which the separation would be LEAST advisable from the standpoint of the child's emotional development is between the ages of _____ months.

   A. 1 and 6
   B. 8 and 16
   C. 16 and 20
   D. 20 and 24

24. Of the following, the term to which empathy is LEAST related is

   A. sublimation
   B. identification
   C. introjection
   D. projection

KEY (CORRECT ANSWERS)

1. C
2. B
3. B
4. B
5. B

6. C
7. A
8. C
9. D
10. A

11. B
12. A
13. D
14. B
15. D

16. C
17. B
18. A
19. C
20. A

21. A
22. C
23. B
24. A

———

EXAMINATION SECTION
TEST 1

DIRECTIONS: Each question or incomplete statement is followed by several suggested answers or completions. Select the one that BEST answers the question or completes the statement. *PRINT THE LETTER OF THE CORRECT ANSWER IN THE SPACE AT THE RIGHT.*

1. Epilepsy is MAINLY associated with   1.____

    A. brain injury B. migraine
    C. dysrhythmia D. aggressivity

2. A disturbance of language perception and expression is called   2.____

    A. aphasia B. amnesia C. amentia D. alexia

3. Alcoholism is MOST commonly connected with   3.____

    A. dysrhythmia B. neurosis
    C. psychopathy D. overt homosexuality

4. The polygraph is MOST useful for diagnosing   4.____

    A. epilepsy B. aggressivity
    C. deception D. brain damage

5. The electroencephalogram is MOST useful for diagnosing   5.____

    A. brain tumor B. epilepsy
    C. brain injury D. mental deficiency

6. Shock therapy was recommended for   6.____

    A. paranoid schizophrenics B. depressed psychotics
    C. severe psychoneurotics D. psychopaths

7. Prefrontal lobotomy had been recommended for   7.____

    A. aggressive psychotics B. apathetic psychotics
    C. paranoid psychotics D. psychopaths

8. Most authorities believe that mental deficiency is _____ hereditary.   8.____

    A. never B. always C. sometimes D. rarely

9. Recent experiments utilizing glutamic acid in an attempt to raise the intellectual level of retarded children have resulted in   9.____

    A. inconclusive findings
    B. a marked temporary rise in intellectual level
    C. a marked permanent rise in intellectual level
    D. a slight temporary decline in intellectual level

10. An individual's Rorschach protocol may be MOST profitably interpreted in the light of his   10.____

    A. behavior while being tested B. case history
    C. other test results D. presenting problems

35

11. If a child is mentally retarded, his academic potential can be explained MOST readily to his parent in terms of the status of other children

    A. in his class
    B. of similar CA
    C. of similar MA
    D. of similar IQ

12. It is MOST probable that a school-age child characterized, on the basis of psychological tests, as a mental defective might, in fact, be

    A. epileptic
    B. deaf
    C. mute
    D. schizophrenic

13. The classroom behavior MOST characteristic of the brain injured child includes

    A. distractibility, hyperactivity, and lack of inhibition
    B. listlessness, withdrawal, and compulsiveness
    C. aggressiveness, fearfulness, and egocentrism
    D. perseveration, fatigue, and apathy

14. A child's MOST rapid rate of mental growth generally occurs

    A. during the first few months of life
    B. between the ages of 3-6
    C. between the ages of 6-12
    D. during early adolescence

15. A psychopath may be distinguished by the fact that he commits antisocial acts

    A. consistently
    B. without customary reaction to guilt
    C. without awareness of what he is doing
    D. violently

16. Of the following techniques, the one which is considered to be characteristic of non-directive or client-centered therapy is

    A. encouraging transference
    B. reflection of feeling
    C. free association
    D. permissive questioning

17. Psychoanalytic writers consider the MOST important aspect of an analyst's training to be his

    A. training in psychoanalytic concepts
    B. training in medicine
    C. training in analysis
    D. general psychological training

18. In the transference situation, it is MOST probable that there will be _____ feeling(s) between analyst and patient.

    A. positive
    B. negative
    C. neutral
    D. positive and negative

19. The sequelae of encephalitis

    A. are now preventable in virtually every case of the disease
    B. may become evident long after an acute attack of the disease
    C. respond readily to treatment when detected
    D. are physical and emotional but rarely mental

20. The mental mechanism most strongly EMPHASIZED in psychoanalytic formulations of schizophrenia is

    A. repression
    B. conversion
    C. projection
    D. regression

21. Paranoia differs from the paranoid type of schizophrenia in

    A. the occurrence of delusions in one and not the other
    B. the fact that the paranoid patient does not act on the basis of his delusions
    C. the amount of *psychopathic tainting* in the family history
    D. that the delusions are more systematized

22. According to the Freudian psychoanalysts, the personality changes in general paresis are due to

    A. oedipus complex
    B. infantile sex urges
    C. sublimations
    D. changes in narcissism

23. A patient who touched his chin when asked to touch his nose would be MOST likely to be suffering from

    A. motor apraxia
    B. motor ataxia
    C. sensory apraxia
    D. agnosia

24. Shock treatment for schizophrenia, especially by the use of metrazol, was introduced at first because of the theory that

    A. shock arouses special physiological defense mechanisms by way of the *alarm reaction*
    B. shock stimulates the autonomic nervous sytem and thus facilitates homeostasis
    C. convulsions protect epileptics against developing schizophrenic symptoms
    D. shock as a form of punishment gratifies the patient's masochistic tendencies

25. From his survey of experimental evidence on the effect of infant care on later personality, Orlansky was led to the conclusion that such factors as breastfeeding and toilet-training

    A. are of no significance for later personality
    B. are significant determiners of personality
    C. are relevant to personality only insofar as they indicate the mother's attitude, which is the effective factor
    D. may help determine personality but constitutional and post-infantile factors should receive major emphasis

KEY (CORRECT ANSWERS)

1. C
2. A
3. B
4. C
5. B

6. B
7. A
8. C
9. A
10. B

11. C
12. D
13. A
14. A
15. B

16. B
17. C
18. D
19. B
20. D

21. D
22. D
23. A
24. C
25. D

TEST 2

DIRECTIONS: Each question or incomplete statement is followed by several suggested answers or completions. Select the one that BEST answers the question or completes the statement. *PRINT THE LETTER OF THE CORRECT ANSWER IN THE SPACE AT THE RIGHT.*

1. A part of the nervous system NOT known to have any connection with emotional behavior is referred to as the   1._____

    A. parasympathetic nervous system
    B. basal ganglia
    C. frontal lobes of cerebral cortex
    D. temporal lobes of cerebral cortex

2. A phobia is _____ anxiety.   2._____

    A. less specific than   B. more specific than
    C. synonymous with an   D. less acute than

3. The division of the autonomic nervous system that coordinates bodily changes in fear and anger is   3._____

    A. sacral   B. sympathetic
    C. emergency   D. cranial

4. The effect of familiarity in the case of inter-racial attitudes is   4._____

    A. dependent upon the nature of the contact
    B. a tendency to breed contempt
    C. greater understanding and acceptance
    D. of little importance one way or the other

5. Negativism is MOST typical of children at the age of _____ year(s).   5._____

    A. one   B. three   C. six   D. nine

6. Children's groups about the age of two typically show   6._____

    A. much cooperation   B. sex segregation
    C. parallel activity   D. none of the above

7. In which of the following functions does development depend MOST completely upon maturation?   7._____

    A. Roller skating   B. Swimming
    C. Singing   D. Walking

8. In the first months of an infant's life, the baby's reflex responses are   8._____

    A. almost the only reactions the baby shows
    B. virtually absent from behavior
    C. more accurate than later in life
    D. less conspicuous than generalized mass reactions

9. Play and reading interests of boys and girls will be found to be most DIFFERENT at the age of _____ years.

   A. three B. six C. twelve D. eighteen

10. The unsociability often reported for very bright children is MOST likely to be due to

   A. their biological makeup
   B. their complete absorption in intellectual pursuits
   C. their lack of personal attractiveness
   D. the absence of suitable companions

11. If we measure a number of individuals upon a variety of complex mental functions, we will find that the different functions show _____ relationship.

   A. a negative
   B. no
   C. a fairly high degree of positive
   D. practically a perfect positive

12. Of the following general statements about deterioration in mental patients, which is the MOST questionable at present?

   A. More recently acquired forms of reaction are lost before those formed earlier in life.
   B. Generalization and abstraction in psychoses is qualitatively the same as that in the young child.
   C. Deterioration in many cases regarded as hopeless appears to be reversible.
   D. The responses of a deteriorated person show generally a definite patterning which tends to mask his defects.

13. Concerning the course of intellectual deterioration in the mental disorders, it is CORRECT to state that

   A. defect in the ability to generalize is more characteristic of schizophrenia than of other psychotic states
   B. concept formation deteriorates more slowly in schizophrenia than in senile psychosis
   C. decreased speed and persistence in mental activity are characteristic of epilepsy
   D. senile patients suffer more impairment in the recall of long past events than in recent memory

14. According to mental test comparisons of cooperative patients in the various disease groups, the group which shows the LEAST intellectual impairment is

   A. paranoid schizophrenia B. psychopathic personality
   C. hebephrenic schizophrenia D. hysteria

15. Schizophrenic speech is BEST characterized by

   A. loose, approximate use of words and reaction to superficial similarities among ideas and objects
   B. loose, approximate use of words and failure to make use of similarities or analogies

C. unusual amount of stammering and reaction to superficial similarities among ideas and objects
D. unusual amount of stammering and failure to make use of similarities or analogies

16. It is the central, distinguishing feature of the depressive phase of manic-depressive psychosis that the patient

    A. is keenly aware of lacking a motive for existence
    B. attaches his depression to some irrelevant or imaginary cause
    C. is excessively disturbed over some recent trouble
    D. is overactive, restless, and even agitated

17. In which of the following abilities do dull and gifted children tend to differ most markedly?

    A. Arithmetical computation
    B. Drawing
    C. Reading comprehension
    D. Spelling

18. The schizophrenic patient is said to exhibit loss of affect. This amounts to

    A. decreased attention to one's personal feeling tone
    B. lack of emotional reaction toward abstract ideas
    C. increased affectivity to ideas and decreased affectivity concerning persons and events
    D. increased affectiveness in environment but less to abstractions

19. Ability to establish a conditioned response in the eyelid has been found to be a point of differentiation between

    A. idiopathic epilepsy and hysterical seizures
    B. malingering and traumatic neurosis
    C. senile dementia and cerebral arteriosclerosis
    D. hysterical and organic blindness

20. The MAIN distinction between normal grief and reactive neurosis is in the

    A. feelings of inadequacy and unreality
    B. lack of basis in real occurrence
    C. duration and intensity of the emotional display
    D. intellectual retardation

21. Kretschmer's dysplastic type applies to those with

    A. compact, round, fleshy habitus
    B. strong, solid, muscular build
    C. slender bodies, long bones, little muscular strength
    D. conspicuous disharmony due to abnormal functioning of the endocrine glands

22. Which of the following is NOT characteristic of anxiety neurosis? 22.____

    A. Increase of irritable tension
    B. Vague somatic complaints
    C. Hypersensitivity to external stimuli
    D. Temporary muscular paralysis of the limbs

23. Involutional melancholia is usually characterized by a 23.____

    A. marked motor agitation   B. motor depression
    C. flight of ideas   D. loss of affect

24. From our knowledge about hallucinatory phenomena, it can be stated reliably that 24.____

    A. hallucinations occur in association with a dreamlike state
    B. hallucinations and imagery are similar processes differing only in intensity
    C. mescal-induced hallucinations are not similar to schizophrenic hallucinations
    D. organized hallucinations can be produced by direct stimulation of the brain surface

25. Which of the following is NOT a form of epilepsy? 25.____

    A. Grand mal   B. Pyknolepsy
    C. Jacksonian   D. Parkinsonian

KEY (CORRECT ANSWERS)

1. B
2. B
3. D
4. A
5. B
6. C
7. D
8. D
9. C
10. D
11. C
12. B
13. A
14. A
15. A
16. A
17. C
18. C
19. D
20. C
21. D
22. D
23. A
24. D
25. D

EXAMINATION SECTION
TEST 1

DIRECTIONS: Each question or incomplete statement is followed by several suggested answers or completions. Select the one that BEST answers the question or completes the statement. *PRINT THE LETTER OF THE CORRECT ANSWER IN THE SPACE AT THE RIGHT.*

1. A patient tells you that the other patients are plotting to kill him. This is MOST likely an example of

    A. a manic-depressive reaction
    B. a paranoid reaction
    C. excellent perceptual skills on the part of the patient
    D. a compulsive reaction

2. Which of the following statements is TRUE?

    A. Diagnoses are, by their very nature, always accurate.
    B. Phobic reactions are the most common reasons people are admitted to mental hospitals.
    C. People with neuroses are far less likely to be hospitalized than people with psychoses.
    D. Severely depressed patients are less of a suicide risk than any other patient group, except paranoid schizophrenics.

3. The LARGEST single diagnostic group of psychotic patients are

    A. neurotic depressive   B. schizophrenic
    C. obsessive-compulsive   D. paranoid reactive

4. The personality type that would BEST be characterized by the description that *he or she has no conscience* would be the

    A. drug addict   B. exhibitionist
    C. sociopath   D. manic-depressive

5. Of the following, the marked inability to organize one's thoughts is found MOST commonly and severely in

    A. schizophrenics
    B. amnesiacs
    C. those suffering from anxiety neuroses
    D. sociopaths

6. Someone who constantly feels tense, anxious, and worried but is unable to identify exactly why is MOST likely to be suffering from

    A. anxiety neurosis   B. schizophrenia
    C. dissociative reaction   D. a conversion reaction

7. A patient always insists upon twirling around six times before entering a new room, or she fears she will die. This is an example of

    A. paranoid reaction   B. obsessive-compulsive reaction
    C. dissociative reaction   D. anxiety neurosis

8. Of the following, those who suffer from neuroses would USUALLY complain of

   A. rejections, dissociation, and frequent inability to remember what day it is
   B. delusions, rejections, and feeling tired
   C. tiredness, fears, and hallucinations
   D. fears, physical complaints, and anxieties

9. The category that is caused by a disorder of the brain for which physical pathology can be demonstrated is

   A. neurotic depressive reaction
   B. schizophrenia
   C. functional psychoses
   D. organic psychoses

10. Of the following, which is NOT true?

    A. Someone who is suddenly unable to hear for psychological reasons would be considered to be suffering from a conversion reaction.
    B. If someone is in fugue, they have combined amnesia with flight.
    C. *Multiple personalities* is a dissociative reaction that affects primarily the elderly.
    D. General symptoms of schizophrenia include an ability to deal with reality, the presence of delusions or hallucinations, and inappropriate affect.

11. Which one of the following is TRUE?

    A. Calling an elderly person *gramps* or *granny* makes them feel more secure.
    B. It is important for an elderly person to maintain his or her independence whenever possible.
    C. When elderly patients start acting like children, they should be treated like children.
    D. It is important to encourage the elderly to hurry because they tend to move so slowly.

12. It has been found that older patients learn BEST when one does all but which one of the following?

    A. Allowing plenty of time for them to practice and learn
    B. Creating a relaxing environment for them
    C. Dealing with one thing at a time
    D. Assuming little knowledge on their part

13. Which of the following contains the main factors that should be considered before administering medications to elderly patients?

    A. How popular the medication is with the patient and the team leader's recommendations
    B. Any organic brain damage, liver dysfunction, and body weight
    C. Liver dysfunction, the patient's medical history, and decreased body weight
    D. Decreased body weight, impaired circulation, liver dysfunction, and increased sensitivity to medications

14. When communicating with the hearing impaired, it is BEST to do all of the following EXCEPT

    A. make sure the person can see your lips
    B. speak slowly and clearly
    C. use gestures
    D. shout

15. The three most common visual disorders in the elderly are cataracts, diabetic retinopathy, and glaucoma.
    Of the following statements about these, the one that is NOT true is that

    A. the symptoms for cataracts are a need for brighter light and a need to hold things very near the eyes
    B. diabetic retinopathy, if untreated, can cause blindness, so any vision or eye problems in diabetics should be promptly reported
    C. glaucoma develops slowly, so it is much easier to detect than cataracts or diabetic retinopathy
    D. some of the symptoms of glaucoma are loss of vision out of the corner of the eye, headaches, nausea, eye pain, tearing, blurred vision, and halos around objects of light

16. Which of the following is NOT true?

    A. Most of the elderly hospitalized for psychiatric problems suffer from senile brain atrophy or brain changes that occur due to arteriosclerosis.
    B. It is important to allow the elderly who wish to, the right to always live in the past.
    C. The majority of the elderly are competent, alert, and functioning well in their communities.
    D. Many elderly patients feel that they are no longer valued members of our society.

17. Of the following, which is NOT a good reason for helping the elderly patient stay active? Activity

    A. promotes good health by stimulating appetite and regulating bowel function
    B. prevents the complications of inactivity such as pneumonia, bed sores, and joint immobility
    C. can create an interest in taking more medication
    D. can increase blood circulation

18. Staff members must come to an understanding of their own feelings about the elderly because

    A. the staff may then be more helpful
    B. any negative feelings one has may be difficult to hide
    C. feelings of fear or aversion can be easily transmitted
    D. all of the above

19. An elderly patient will probably eat better if

   A. food servings are large
   B. the foods are chewy
   C. he or she is allowed to finish his/her meals at a leisurely pace
   D. cooked food is served cold

20. The MOST common accident to the elderly involves

   A. falls   B. burns   C. bruises   D. cuts

21. Which of the following is TRUE?

   A. Children should be considered and treated as miniature adults.
   B. Children are growing, developing human beings who will react to situations according to their level of development and the experiences to which they have been subjected.
   C. Children who are brought to a mental health center are usually calm and non-apprehensive on their first visit.
   D. The problems of adolescents are usually overestimated.

22. In working with adolescents, it would be BEST to

   A. neither bend over backwards to give in to demands, nor control them by rigid and punitive means
   B. dress the way most adolescents do
   C. staff those units with young people
   D. watch television with them regularly

23. Of the following, when working with children, it is MOST important to be

   A. consistent
   B. strict
   C. more concerned for their welfare than for the welfare of the other patients
   D. well-liked

24. Of the following, the element that is MOST lacking in relationships between adolescents and adults is

   A. respect   B. fear   C. trust   D. sensitivity

25. Of the following, the BEST reason for grouping children together would be

   A. they should be protected from the influences of all adult patients
   B. children tend to feel more comfortable with other children
   C. children are less likely to *act out* when they are with other children
   D. they would be unable to bother adult patients

26. All of the following statements are true EXCEPT:

    A. Accidents, reactions to drugs, fevers, and disease may each contribute to mental or emotional problems
    B. How effectively an individual reacts to and manages stress contributes to his or her mental health
    C. There is significant research that indicates that mental illness is caused primarily by genetic transmittal
    D. A person's upbringing, his or her relationships with family or friends, past experiences, and present living conditions may all contribute to the status of his or her mental health

27. All of the following are basic psychological needs which must be met for a person to have self-esteem EXCEPT

    A. acceptance and understanding
    B. trust, respect, and security
    C. a rewarding romantic relationship
    D. pleasant interactions with other people

28. All of the following statements are true EXCEPT:

    A. Most people become mentally ill because they are unable to cope with or adapt to the stresses and problems of life
    B. People with emotional problems can rarely be helped enough to live independently
    C. Most of the diseases and symptoms of the body which plague people have a large emotional component as their cause
    D. Environmental and familial factors are more important than genetic factors in mental illness

29. The following are all optimal aspects of family functioning EXCEPT

    A. communication is open and direct
    B. expression of emotion is more often positive than negative
    C. minor problems are ignored, knowing they will go away on their own
    D. there is a high degree of congruence or harmony between the family's values and the actual realities of the society

30. All of the following statements are true EXCEPT:

    A. People who are wealthy rarely become mentally ill
    B. Physical disease may influence emotional balance
    C. People who are mentally ill are often very sensitive to what is happening in their environment
    D. Most people doubt their own sanity at one time or another

31. All of the following statements are true EXCEPT:

    A. Hereditary factors are not the primary cause of mental illness
    B. A person may react to an extremely traumatic experience by becoming mentally ill
    C. Early recognition and treatment does not affect the course of mental illness
    D. Mental illness can develop suddenly

32. All of the following statements are true EXCEPT:

    A. Emotionally disturbed people are usually very sensitive to how other people feel towards them
    B. People do not inherit mental disorders, but may inherit a predisposition to certain types of mental problems
    C. There are many factors which can cause mental illness
    D. Mood swings are signs of mental illness

33. Which of the following statements is LEAST accurate?

    A. The difference between being mentally healthy and mentally ill often lies in the intensity and frequency of inappropriate behavior.
    B. The way a person views a situation determines his or her response to the situation.
    C. The mentally ill are permanently disabled.
    D. Different personal experiences cause a difference in what a person perceives as stressful, and how much stress a person can tolerate.

34. All of the following statements are true EXCEPT:

    A. Most experts in the field of mental health believe that the experiences which occur during the first twenty, or the first six, years of life are the most significant
    B. An unfortunate characteristic of children is that they tend to blame themselves for failures of their parents, and thus may develop feelings of inadequacy which may affect them all of their lives
    C. If neglect is severe enough, an infant or young child may withdraw from reality into a fantasy world which feels less threatening
    D. Human beings develop in the exact same pattern and almost at the same rate

35. Schizophrenia is

    A. genetically caused
    B. most often caused by the habitual use of drugs
    C. the result of a complex relationship between biological, psychological, and sociological factors
    D. most commonly caused by the inhalation of toxic gases

KEY (CORRECT ANSWERS)

1.	B		16.	B
2.	C		17.	C
3.	B		18.	D
4.	C		19.	C
5.	A		20.	A
6.	A		21.	B
7.	B		22.	A
8.	D		23.	A
9.	D		24.	C
10.	C		25.	B
11.	B		26.	C
12.	D		27.	C
13.	D		28.	B
14.	D		29.	C
15.	C		30.	A

31. C
32. D
33. C
34. D
35. C

TEST 2

DIRECTIONS: Each question or incomplete statement is followed by several suggested answers or completions. Select the one that BEST answers the question or completes the statement. *PRINT THE LETTER OF THE CORRECT ANSWER IN THE SPACE AT THE RIGHT.*

1. Tardive dyskenesia is a(n)

    A. antidepressant
    B. birth-related serious injury
    C. serious side effect of phenothiazine derivatives
    D. antiparkinsons drug

    1.____

2. People taking psychotropic drugs are MOST likely to be sensitive to

    A. long exposures to sunlight
    B. darkness
    C. noise
    D. other patients

    2.____

3. An antipsychotic drug that is a phenothiazine derivative would MOST likely be used for

    A. helping a patient lose weight
    B. calming a patient
    C. helping a patient sleep
    D. reducing the frequency of delusions in a patient

    3.____

4. Of the following, an antidepressant such as Elavil would MOST likely be used for

    A. the immediate prevention of suicidal action in a newly admitted patient
    B. helping a patient lose weight
    C. elevating a patient's mood
    D. diuretic purposes

    4.____

5. Which of the following statements is NOT true?

    A. Antianxiety tranquilizers such as sparine, librium, and vistaril are useful primarily with psychoneurotic and psychosomatic disorders.
    B. Minor or antianxiety tranquilizers tend to be less habit-forming than major or antipsychotic tranquilizers.
    C. Akinesia, pseudoparkinsonism, and tardive dyskenesia are serious side effects of antipsychotic drugs, or phenothiazine derivatives.
    D. Generally, those using tranquilizers like sparine or librium are in less danger of deadly drug overdoses than those using barbituates.

    5.____

6. All of the following statements are false EXCEPT:

    A. Antipsychotic drugs promote increased sexual interest
    B. Patients no longer need to take their medication when they feel better
    C. Phenothiazines are psychotropic drugs
    D. One of the main difficulties with antipsychotic drugs is that they tend to be habit-forming

    6.____

7. Yellowing of the skin or eyes, sensitivity to light and pseudoparkinsonism may occur in patients receiving

   A. mellaril or thorazine
   B. librium or tranxene
   C. valium or vistaril
   D. antiparkinson drugs

8. Which of the following is NOT true of extrapyramidal symptoms (EPS)? They

   A. may appear after many weeks of use of phenothiazines
   B. can safely be controlled without medical assistance
   C. may appear after the patient has been taking the drug for only a few days
   D. may include pseudoparkinsonism

9. The time required to reach an effective blood level for an antidepressant medication would MOST likely be three

   A. days   B. hours   C. weeks   D. months

10. An example of a psychotropic drug would be

    A. seconal   B. aspirin   C. librium   D. perichloz

11. In evaluating a patient you are meeting for the first time, it would be best NOT to

    A. be as objective as possible
    B. question one's own motives and reactions when processing data during and after the meeting
    C. be extremely goal-oriented
    D. not allow any praise or criticism directed at you by the patient to influence your assessment

12. All of the following statements are true EXCEPT:

    A. People communicate non-verbally via their behavior and their body posture
    B. Non-verbal clues may be a better indication of a patient's true feelings than what the patient actually says
    C. A patient who is highly anxious is easier to evaluate than a patient who is relatively calm
    D. People should be judged objectively

13. When asking a patient a question, one should do all of the following EXCEPT

    A. phrase questions in order to receive a yes or no response
    B. ask only relevant questions
    C. listen carefully to the response before asking the next question
    D. phrase questions clearly

14. The MAIN purpose for extensive record keeping is to

    A. provide an accurate description of the patient's diagnosis
    B. provide a subjective report of the patient's behavior
    C. provide an objective report of the patient's behavior
    D. give mental health personnel something to do

15. When talking to a patient for the first time, one must realize that

    A. hostile behavior indicates an extremely severe disorder in the patient
    B. a patient's physical appearance will indicate how successful you will be in communicating with the patient
    C. the patient is extremely nervous
    D. you are both strangers to each other

16. Of the following, which statement is NOT true?

    A. The rapid assessment of a patient is not necessarily accomplished by asking a series of routine questions.
    B. There is value, in assessing a patient, in creating a conversational bridge which has *here and now* relevance.
    C. One can assess a patient's state by his or her reaction to a warm greeting given to him or her.
    D. There is some value in routinely asking certain questions, when needed, in order to check a patient's orientation and memory.

17. All of the following could be signs that someone is moving towards mental illness EXCEPT

    A. exhibiting a degree of prolonged, constant anxiety, apprehension, or fear which is out of proportion with reality
    B. severe appetite disturbances
    C. occasional depression
    D. abrupt changes in a person's behavior

18. The first few minutes of interaction with a patient can reveal all but

    A. a patient's contact with reality
    B. whether you are comfortable with a patient
    C. a patient's mood
    D. a patient's chances for recovery

19. Which of the following statements is TRUE?

    A. The tentative diagnosis made when a patient is first admitted is the most accurate diagnosis.
    B. One should always try and keep in mind the state the patient was in when first admitted.
    C. A diagnosis is actually an ongoing process.
    D. When assessing patients' behavior, it is best to be suspicious of what may look like progress.

20. All of the following are examples of defense mechanisms EXCEPT

    A. projection
    B. complimenting someone
    C. displacement
    D. regression

21. A treatment plan is likely to be MOST effective if the

    A. patient's suggestions are always incorporated
    B. patient is voluntarily and wholeheartedly participating in the treatment plan designed for him or her

C. patient has daily contact with his or her family
D. patient respects the team leader

22. All of the following are true EXCEPT:

    A. Patients do not become well simply by people doing something for them
    B. A patient's well-being is enhanced when one or more team members can forge a *therapeutic alliance* with that patient
    C. The most important purpose of the treatment team is to administer the proper medications to patients
    D. It is important that a patient be seen as an individual, and not just as a *case* or a *number*

23. Of the following, a member of the treatment team can BEST assist a patient by

    A. commanding respect from other team members
    B. carefully observing the behavior of patients
    C. avoiding spending too much time with patients
    D. becoming friends with a patient

24. Of the following, which is LEAST important when considering a treatment plan?

    A. Involving the patient
    B. Setting reasonable goals
    C. Being as specific as possible in setting completion dates for goals, and sticking to them
    D. Detailing the methods to be followed, and the work assignments

25. All of the following are true EXCEPT:

    A. A treatment team should help patients understand that they can improve their condition if they will cooperate with the treatment plan
    B. Patients should be encouraged to participate in the programs designed for them
    C. Patients should be encouraged to revise their treatment plans
    D. One's approach should be tailored for each individual, whenever possible

26. All of the following could be considered appropriate goals for patients to work towards, EXCEPT to

    A. expand one's capacity to find or create acceptable options
    B. learn to be less dependent
    C. give up feeling persecuted
    D. learn how to get what one needs, at any cost

27. In working in treatment teams, it is MOST important for team members to

    A. communicate effectively with each other
    B. enjoy working with each other
    C. keep morale high
    D. attend meetings on time

28. One of the purposes of the treatment team is to

   A. decrease the amount of work
   B. coordinate and integrate services to patients
   C. provide training
   D. provide patients with basic counseling skills they can use

29. When working with someone exhibiting a manic-depressive psychosis, depressed type, it is BEST to

   A. concern yourself primarily with his or her eating habits
   B. focus primarily on their sleeping habits
   C. take every statement he or she may make about suicide seriously
   D. allow them to watch a great deal of television

30. In working with a paranoid patient, all of the following are true EXCEPT: It

   A. is important to listen with respect
   B. is helpful to establish a trusting relationship
   C. is good to try and talk the patient out of his or her fears
   D. would not be a good practice to agree with their statements, if they are not true

31. It is important, when dealing with verbally abusive patients, to keep in mind all of the following EXCEPT:

   A. Patients usually become abusive because of frustrating circumstances beyond their control
   B. In most cases, the patients do not mean anything personal by their abusive remarks; they are displacing anger
   C. It is important for staff members to remain calm and controlled when patients have emotional outbursts
   D. It is a good idea to allow an angry patient to draw you into an argument, as this will eventually help calm him or her down

32. When dealing with a patient who insists upon doing a number of rituals before brushing his teeth, it would be BEST to

   A. attempt to tease him out of his behavior
   B. not be critical of the ritualistic behavior
   C. perform the same rituals so that he feels more secure
   D. insist that he eliminate one step of the ritual each week

33. A patient tells you that he is balancing an automobile on the top of his head, and asks you what you think of that.
   An APPROPRIATE response for you to make would be:

   A. to ask him to take you for a ride
   B. *Stop saying ridiculous things*
   C. *I know you believe you are balancing a car on your head but I don't see it, therefore I have to assume that you're not*
   D. *Is it an invisible car*

34. A new patient, who is very paranoid, refuses to take off his clothes before getting into bed.
    Which would be MOST helpful?

    A. Getting another staff member to assist in removing his clothes
    B. Leaving the room until he comes to his senses
    C. Trying to find out why the patient does not want to undress
    D. Allowing the patient to stay up all night

35. In handling depressed patients, it is BEST to

    A. encourage them to participate in activities
    B. remind them often that things will be better tomorrow
    C. remember that depressed patients have few feelings of guilt
    D. let them know that you know just how they are feeling

36. A patient tells you that she is very depressed over the recent death of her brother. Which of the following would be the MOST appropriate response?

    A. *Everybody gets depressed when they lose someone they love.*
    B. *It could have been worse; at least he was ill only a short time.*
    C. *I know just how you feel.*
    D. *This must be very difficult for you.*

37. A patient who recently suffered a stroke refuses to let you help her bathe.
    This is probably because

    A. it is hard for her to accept that she can no longer do things for herself that she could do before the stroke
    B. she does not like you
    C. she is extremely independent and should be encouraged to be less so
    D. you need to review your methods for bathing patients

38. All of the following would be appropriate in working with a patient who is hallucinating EXCEPT

    A. carefully watch what you are non-verbally communicating
    B. ask concrete, reality-oriented questions
    C. provide a calm, structured environment
    D. agree with the patient, if asked, that you are experiencing the same state he or she is

39. In dealing with overactive patients, it is BEST to

    A. not give most of your attention to these patients, leaving the quieter patients to look after themselves
    B. keep in mind that overactive patients are always more interesting than other patients
    C. remember that overactive patients need more care than other patients
    D. forcibly restrain them whenever possible

40. A patient with mild organic brain damage is very withdrawn and negativistic. 40.____
 The BEST approach, of the following, would be

   A. *I need a partner to play cards with me*
   B. *Your family is very disappointed in you when you act like this*
   C. *Your doctor said you should participate in all activities here, so you'd better do that*
   D. *Would you like to go to your room so you can be alone?*

KEY (CORRECT ANSWERS)

1. C	11. C	21. B	31. D
2. A	12. C	22. C	32. B
3. D	13. A	23. B	33. C
4. C	14. C	24. C	34. C
5. B	15. D	25. C	35. A
6. C	16. C	26. D	36. D
7. A	17. C	27. A	37. A
8. B	18. D	28. B	38. D
9. C	19. C	29. C	39. A
10. C	20. B	30. C	40. A

EXAMINATION SECTION
TEST 1

DIRECTIONS: Each question or incomplete statement is followed by several suggested answers or completions. Select the one that BEST answers the question or completes the statement. *PRINT THE LETTER OF THE CORRECT ANSWER IN THE SPACE AT THE RIGHT.*

1. The causes of abnormal behavior include

    A. alcohol and drugs
    B. head injuries and severe infection
    C. diabetes and psychiatric problems
    D. all of the above

    1.____

2. All of the following are common reactions to anxiety EXCEPT

    A. depression
    B. flight of ideas
    C. denial
    D. regression

    2.____

3. Of the following infections, the one which does NOT produce psychotic syndrome is

    A. chancroid
    B. brain abscess
    C. syphilis
    D. toxoplasmosis

    3.____

4. In dealing with emotionally disturbed patients, an EMT should

    A. not assess the patient's needs
    B. intervene in the situation to the extent to which he feels capable
    C. overreact to the patient's behavior or emotional attacks
    D. none of the above

    4.____

5. Crisis situations, including periods of _____, may affect the paramedic adversely.

    A. anxiety
    B. anger
    C. impatience
    D. all of the above

    5.____

6. A professional attitude MUST be maintained while the paramedic is dealing with emotionally disturbed patients. This attitude can be characterized by all of the following EXCEPT

    A. anger
    B. warmth
    C. sensitivity
    D. compassion

    6.____

7. The common emotional difficulties of the paramedic may be managed by

    A. discussing problems and anxieties with co-workers
    B. developing a regular discussion rap session with peers to discuss good and bad experiences
    C. discussing problems with the supervisor
    D. all of the above

    7.____

8. There are certain general guidelines for dealing with any patient with a psychiatric problem.
   The one of the following which is NOT among these guidelines is:

   A. Be prepared to spend time with the disturbed patient.
   B. Be as calm and direct as possibl
   C. You do not need to identify yoursel
   D. Assess the patient wherever the emergency occurs.

9. Disorders of motor activity include all of the following EXCEPT

   A. agitation
   B. compulsion
   C. perservation
   D. restlessness

10. A repetitive action carried out to relieve the anxiety of obsessive thought is called

    A. compulsion
    B. delirium
    C. confrontation
    D. confabulation

11. The invention of experiences to cover over gaps in memory, seen in patients with certain organic brain syndromes, is

    A. dementia
    B. confabulation
    C. psychosis
    D. delusion

12. Among the following, which is NOT a symptom of a panic attack?

    A. Shortness of breath or a sensation of being smothered
    B. Feeling of unreality or of stepping apart from oneself
    C. Constant fatigue and no motivation to do anything
    D. Fear of dying and of being crazy

13. Risk factors for violence do NOT include

    A. any place where alcohol is being consumed
    B. natural death in the family
    C. crowd incidents
    D. incidents where violence has already occurred (e.g., shooting, stabbing)

14. Disorders of thinking include all of the following EXCEPT

    A. flight of ideas
    B. retardation of thought
    C. compulsions
    D. perseveration

15. All of the following are disorders of consciousness EXCEPT

    A. amnesia
    B. delirium
    C. fugue stage
    D. stupor and coma

16. A repetition of movements that don,t seem to serve any useful purpose is called

    A. compulsion
    B. echolalia
    C. stereotyped activity
    D. all of the above

17. The definition of *compulsion* is:

    A. A repetitive action carried out to relieve the anxiety of obsessive thought
    B. The situation in which a patient cannot sit still
    C. Condition in which the patient echoes the words of the examiner
    D. None of the above

18. The MOST profound disorder of memory is

    A. confabulation   B. amnesia
    C. illusion   D. hallucination

19. An acute state of confusion characterized by global impairment of thinking, perception, and memory is called

    A. delusion   B. delirium   C. psychosis   D. dementia

20. Proper pre-hospital management of the manic patient includes

    A. not arguing or getting into a power struggle with the patient
    B. talking to a patient in a quiet place, away from other people
    C. consulting medical command if the patient refuses transport
    D. all of the above

Questions 21-25.

DIRECTIONS: In Questions 21 through 25, match the numbered definition with the lettered disorder, listed in Column I, that it MOST accurately describes. Place the letter of the CORRECT answer in the appropriate space at the right.

COLUMN I
A. Echolalia
B. Illusion
C. Delusion
D. Hallucination
E. Mood

21. Misinterpretation of sensory stimuli

22. False belief

23. Meaningless echoing of the interviewer's words by the patient

24. Sustained and pervasive emotional state

25. Sense of perception not founded on objective reality

KEY (CORRECT ANSWERS)

1.	D		11.	B
2.	B		12.	C
3.	A		13.	B
4.	B		14.	C
5.	D		15.	A
6.	A		16.	C
7.	D		17.	A
8.	C		18.	B
9.	C		19.	B
10.	A		20.	D

21. B
22. C
23. A
24. E
25. D

TEST 2

DIRECTIONS: Each question or incomplete statement is followed by several suggested answers or completions. Select the one that BEST answers the question or completes the statement. *PRINT THE LETTER OF THE CORRECT ANSWER IN THE SPACE AT THE RIGHT.*

1. The depressed patient can often be readily identified by   1.____

    A. a sad expression
    B. bouts of crying
    C. expression of feelings of worthlessness
    D. all of the above

2. The third leading cause of death among the 15- to 25 year-old age group is   2.____

    A. diabetes mellitus   B. rheumatoid arthritis
    C. suicide   D. congenital heart disease

3. The assessment of every depressed person MUST include an evaluation of   3.____

    A. schizophrenia
    B. suicide risk
    C. chronic debilitating illness
    D. anxiety

4. When caring for a patient who is displaying typical stress reactions, you should   4.____

    A. act in a calm manner, giving the patient time to gain control of his emotions
    B. quietly and carefully evaluate the situation
    C. stay alert for sudden changes in behavior
    D. all of the above

5. The patient in a psychiatric emergency is far more out of reach and out of control than   5.____
the person in an emotional emergency.
In a psychiatric emergency, the patient may do all of the following EXCEPT

    A. try to hurt himself
    B. try to seek help for protection
    C. withdraw, no longer responding to people or to his environment
    D. continue to act depressed, sometimes crying and expressing feelings of worthlessness

6. When a patient is acting as if he may hurt himself or another, you should do all of the following EXCEPT   6.____

    A. alert the police
    B. not isolate yourself from your partner or other sources of help
    C. try to restrain the patient by yourself
    D. always be on the watch for weapons

7. A mental disorder characterized by loss of contact with reality is called   7.____

    A. psychosis   B. dementia
    C. phobia   D. none of the above

8. Anti-psychotic drugs are also called

   A. antidepressants
   B. neuroleptics
   C. anxiolytics
   D. antiepileptics

9. The patient who hears voices commanding him to hurt himself or others must be considered

   A. normal
   B. safe
   C. dangerous
   D. none of the above

10. When in a state of *conversion hysteria,* a person's

    A. reaction may move from extreme anxiety to relative calmness
    B. may transform anxiety to some bodily function
    C. often becomes hysterically blind, deaf, or paralyzed
    D. all of the above

11. Repeating the same idea over and over again is called

    A. perseveration
    B. compulsion
    C. obsession
    D. facilitation

12. _____ is the interviewing technique in which the interviewer encourages the patient to proceed by noncommittal words and gestures.

    A. Echolalia
    B. Facilitation
    C. Affect
    D. None of the above

13. The CHRONIC deterioration of mental function is referred to as

    A. dementia
    B. psychosis
    C. delirium
    D. schizophrenia

14. A persistent idea that a person CANNOT dismiss from his thought is a(n)

    A. affect
    B. obsession
    C. compulsion
    D. delusion

15. An interviewing technique in which the interviewer points out to the patient something of interest in his conversation or behavior is

    A. facilitation
    B. confabulation
    C. confrontation
    D. perseveration

16. It is important for paramedics to be aware of one particular syndrome that may occur in patients taking anti-psychotic medication. This condition is

    A. acute diuresis
    B. acute dystonic reaction
    C. hypertensive crises
    D. none of the above

17. An acute dystonic reaction can be rapidly corrected by

    A. chlorpromazine
    B. prolixin
    C. diphenhydramine
    D. tindal

18. Tranquilizers are also called 18.____

    A. neuroleptics   B. anxiolytics
    C. chinergics   D. stimulants

19. The COMMON symptoms of antipsychotic drugs include 19.____

    A. blurred vision   B. dry mouth
    C. cardiac dysrhythmias   D. all of the above

20. Uncontrolled, disconnected thoughts characterize a disorganized patient who may be 20.____

    A. incoherent or rambling in his speech
    B. wandering aimlessly
    C. dressed inappropriately
    D. all of the above

Questions 21-25.

DIRECTIONS: In Questions 21 through 25, match the numbered definition with the lettered disorder, listed in Column I, that it MOST accurately describes. Place the letter of the CORRECT answer in the appropriate space at the right.

<u>COLUMN I</u>
A. Agitation
B. Agoraphobia
C. Flight of ideas
D. Neologism
E. Confabulation

21. Fear of the marketplace 21.____

22. An invented word that has meaning only to its inventor 22.____

23. The invention of experiences to cover over gaps in memory 23.____

24. Extreme restlessness and anxiety 24.____

25. Accelerated thinking in which the mind skips very rapidly from one thought to the next 25.____

KEY (CORRECT ANSWERS)

1. D
2. C
3. B
4. D
5. B

6. C
7. A
8. B
9. C
10. D

11. A
12. B
13. A
14. B
15. C

16. B
17. C
18. B
19. D
20. D

21. B
22. D
23. E
24. A
25. C

EXAMINATION SECTION
TEST 1

DIRECTIONS: Each question or incomplete statement is followed by several suggested answers or completions. Select the one that BEST answers the question or completes the statement. *PRINT THE LETTER OF THE CORRECT ANSWER IN THE SPACE AT THE RIGHT.*

1. In regard to first aid procedures, priority in treatment should be given FIRST to cases of   1._____

    A. internal poisoning
    B. severe eye injuries
    C. stoppage of breathing
    D. severe bleeding at the neck

2. The American Red Cross advocates that for an insect sting on the neck, the first aider apply to the injured part   2._____

    A. a cut in the skin at the spot to encourage bleeding in order to remove impurities
    B. suction in order to remove the injected toxin
    C. ice applications
    D. hot, wet applications

3. The group of symptoms BEST describing a case of shock is   3._____

    A. extreme thirst, skin dry, breathing deep, pulse irregular
    B. face flushed, pulse full, pupils constricted, nauseous-ness
    C. pulse absent, skin hot, breathing heavy, face ashen
    D. body weakness, skin moist, pupils dilated, breathing shallow

4. According to the American Red Cross, the four types of wounds are   4._____

    A. scrapes, cuts, burns, stabs
    B. punctures, lacerations, incisions, abrasions
    C. friction burns, open blisters, gashes, punctures
    D. scratches, infections, sores, bleeding cuts

5. When administering first aid to a pupil experiencing an epileptic attack, the teacher should FIRST   5._____

    A. loosen clothing about the neck and chest
    B. remove the victim to a room other than a classroom filled with pupils
    C. place an object between the victim's upper and lower teeth on one side of the mouth
    D. apply an ammonia ampule to the victim's nostrils

6. In the execution of the back pressure-arm lift method of artificial respiration, all of the following are correct procedures EXCEPT the one in which the operator   6._____

    A. places the victims in the prone position with the face turned to one side
    B. rocks foward with bent elbows as he exerts pressure at a 70° angle
    C. draws the arms of the victim upward and toward him during the final step of the cycle
    D. repeats the cycle at a steady rate of 12 times per minute

7. In second or third degree burns, all of the following are correct first aid procedures EXCEPT

    A. applying mineral oil to the area
    B. giving fluids by mouth
    C. providing immediate first aid for shock
    D. covering the burned area with sterile dressing

8. Of the following symptoms a person might display after receiving a blow to the head, the one MOST indicative of serious injury is

    A. pallor
    B. swelling
    C. dizziness
    D. inequality in size of pupils of the eye

9. When reassuring a victim of an accident, of the following, it is MOST advisable to

    A. explain his condition to him as you find it and state you will stay with him
    B. tell him what first aid steps you are going to take and how they will help him
    C. state to the victim that, since there is no doctor around, you will take his place
    D. keep the victim talking about the accident to relieve tension

10. The rate at which artificial respiration should be given to adults is

    A. about 12 times a minute
    B. about 20 times a minute
    C. as fast as you can work
    D. slightly faster than normal breathing

KEY (CORRECT ANSWERS)

1.	D	6.	B
2.	C	7.	A
3.	D	8.	D
4.	B	9.	B
5.	C	10.	A

TEST 2

DIRECTIONS: Each question or incomplete statement is followed by several suggested answers or completions. Select the one that BEST answers the question or completes the statement. *PRINT THE LETTER OF THE CORRECT ANSWER IN THE SPACE AT THE RIGHT.*

1. In rendering the mouth-to-mouth method of artificial respiration, the one hand of the operator should

    A. cover the victim's nose and the other hand should be placed on the chest
    B. be on the ground near the victim's shoulder and in such position as to assist the other hand in maintaining equal support of his body weight
    C. hold the victim's jaw up and back and the other hand should pinch the victim's nostrils together
    D. be placed around the victim's mouth and the other hand should hold the nape of the victim's neck rigid

    1.____

2. In the case of a severely burned victim who needs fluids, of the following, it is MOST advisable to give him at fifteen-minute intervals

    A. a full cup of hot tea or hot coffee
    B. a teaspoonful of spirits of ammonia in a glass of water
    C. half-glass doses of one-half teaspoon of table salt and of baking soda in a quart of water
    D. a mild stimulant

    2.____

3. In caring for burns, the first aider should

    A. break the blisters caused by the burn
    B. apply wet dressings to the burned area
    C. apply large amounts of lukewarm water to a chemical burn before treating the burn
    D. remove scorched clothing on or near the burn

    3.____

4. A person, in rendering first aid, should

    A. administer medication internally
    B. apply antiseptics to broken skin
    C. attempt to remove foreign bodies from eyes
    D. use the method of artificial respiration best known to him

    4.____

5. In cases of shock, the first aider should elevate the lower part of the victim's body is

    A. the blood loss is great
    B. he complains of pain at a fracture site in the lower extremity
    C. there is a head injury
    D. breathing is difficult

    5.____

6. When rendering first aid to a diabetic who suddenly becomes confused, incoherent, and faint, the FIRST thing to be done is to

    A. keep him warm and comfortable until a doctor arrives
    B. give him some form of sugar if he can swallow
    C. use a mild stimulant to keep him from losing consciousness
    D. take steps to summon an ambulance

    6.____

7. During the winter months, in cases of first aid care for victims of shock, the first aider should

    A. wrap the victim in excess covering while waiting for the arrival of the doctor
    B. cover the victim sparingly in spite of a possible low temperature
    C. always apply hot water bottles to the victim's body
    D. protect the victim's body so that a flushed condition of the skin appears and is then maintained

8. In order to minimize the possibility of infection, the first aider, when caring for a wound, should

    A. wash the body surface toward the wound before applying a gauze dressing
    B. use soap and clean running tap water on both the wound and its surrounding area
    C. apply a two percent iodine solution as his first step in treating the wound
    D. cover the wound with adhesive tape in order to prevent contact with germs

9. If a particle is on the eyeball, one should NOT

    A. close his eyes for a few minutes in order to allow the tears to wash out the foreign matter
    B. grasp the lashes of the upper lid and draw it out and down over the lower lid in order to dislodge the particle
    C. use an eye dropper in order to flush the eye so that the particle will float out of the eye
    D. examine the eye in order to determine the location of the foreign particle and, when found, remove it from the eyeball by touching lightly with the moistened corner of a clean handkerchief

10. Of the following concerning mouth-to-mouth resuscitation, the operator can BEST be sure that no obstruction exists in the victim's air passage by following his first blowing efforts with a

    A. sharp tilt backward of the victim's head so that the chin points almost directly upward
    B. forceful opening of the victim's mouth as the victim's nostrils are held in a closed position
    C. removal of his mouth by turning his head to the side in order to listen for the return rush of air from the victim's body
    D. removal of mucous and foreign matter in the victim's mouth

KEY (CORRECT ANSWERS)

1.	C	6.	B
2.	C	7.	B
3.	B	8.	B
4.	D	9.	D
5.	A	10.	C

TEST 3

DIRECTIONS: Each question or incomplete statement is followed by several suggested answers or completions. Select the one that BEST answers the question or completes the statement. *PRINT THE LETTER OF THE CORRECT ANSWER IN THE SPACE AT THE RIGHT.*

1. The universal antidote to be administered in poisoning cases if no specific antidote is known consists of

    A. several teaspoonfuls of baking soda in half a glass of water
    B. a large glass of milk diluted with an equal amount of water
    C. one part tea, two parts crumbled burnt toast, one part milk of magnesia
    D. one part milk, one part egg white, one part water

    1.____

2. In the case of severe bleeding from a hand, the first aider should IMMEDIATELY

    A. locate the pressure point above the wound and apply digital pressure at that point
    B. apply pressure directly on the wound with clean gauze or a towel
    C. apply a tourniquet in order to limit the flow of blood from the artery to the wound
    D. locate the pressure point and apply a tourniquet at that point

    2.____

3. The INCORRECT association of first aid bandage and body area of use is

    A. four-tailed bandage - nose
    B. cravat bandage - knee
    C. triangular bandage - head
    D. figure-eight bandage - chest

    3.____

4. With victims of shock, when medical help is not immediate, water should NOT be given to those who have

    A. suffered marked bleeding
    B. burns involving more than ten percent of the body surface
    C. a penetrating abdominal wound
    D. a fracture of the femur

    4.____

5. The MAIN objective in first aid care for a victim of poison by mouth is to

    A. first induce vomiting
    B. dilute the poison
    C. give an antidote
    D. look around for tell-tale evidence of the poison

    5.____

6. The LATEST accepted method (American Red Cross) of administering artificial respiration is known as the _____ method.

    A. back-pressure arm-lift
    B. chest-pressure arm-lift
    C. mouth-to-mouth
    D. prone pressure

    6.____

69

7. All of the following statements regarding first aid care are correct EXCEPT:

   A. Soap and clean water may be used to wash the wounded area in case of minor wounds
   B. A modified back-pressure arm-lift method of artificial respiration is recommended for infants and children under 4 years of age
   C. Direct pressure is recommended for most cases of severe bleeding
   D. Shock victims should be kept slightly cool rather than *toasting* warm with little or no surface covering used on warm days

8. In poisoning, the first aider should induce vomiting for all of the following taken through the mouth EXCEPT

   A. lye
   B. barbiturates
   C. mushrooms
   D. iodine

9. A recommended first aid procedure in the treatment of heat stroke is to

   A. give a stimulant
   B. keep the head lower than the chest
   C. apply external heat to the body
   D. sponge the body with lukewarm water

10. Of the following, the distinctive symptom in cases of heat stroke is

    A. a desire to sleep
    B. nausea
    C. absence of perspiration
    D. dizziness

KEY (CORRECT ANSWERS)

1. C
2. B
3. D
4. C
5. B
6. C
7. B
8. A
9. D
10. C

TEST 4

DIRECTIONS: Each question or incomplete statement is followed by several suggested answers or completions. Select the one that BEST answers the question or completes the statement. *PRINT THE LETTER OF THE CORRECT ANSWER IN THE SPACE AT THE RIGHT.*

1. All of the following are recommended first aid measures for insect bites and stings EXCEPT the application of 1.____

    A. a compress moistened with ammonia water
    B. calamine lotion
    C. ice
    D. light massage in order to remove the sting

2. According to the American Red Cross, the INCORRECT association of type of bandage and injury is 2.____

    A. four-tail bandage - fracture of the jaw
    B. spiral-reverse bandage - wound on the forearm
    C. figure-of-eight bandage - sprained ankle
    D. cravat bandage - eye injury

3. A compound fracture is one in which the bone is 3.____

    A. broken in many pieces
    B. broken with a connecting wound on the surface of the body
    C. twisted apart
    D. broken longitudinally

4. One of the shop workers strikes heavily against the wall. You recognize that he is in a state of shock because of his 4.____

    A. strong pulse
    B. regular but deep breathing
    C. moist, pale skin
    D. high body temperature

5. According to the American Red Cross, first aid care for an individual who gives evidence of possible insulin reaction when there is no other reason to account for the trouble includes the 5.____

    A. usual treatment for shock
    B. giving of candy or sugar to the victim
    C. application of artificial respiration
    D. swallowing of a stimulant

6. In caring for frostbite cases, one should 6.____

    A. apply woolen material to the injured area
    B. rub the injured part with snow
    C. massage the affected part
    D. have the victim soak the injured part in water as hot as possible

7. When applying wet applications to infected wounds, one should AVOID

   A. boiling the water prior to its use
   B. adding salt to the liquid
   C. half-hour periods of application followed by alternate free periods of the same length
   D. having the solution hot

8. According to the American Red Cross, tourniquets may be applied in all of the following situations EXCEPT

   A. when severe bleeding involves an extremity in which large arteries are severed
   B. to individuals who are known to be allergic to a bee or wasp sting, if the sting is on an extremity
   C. in cases where there is partial severance of a body part accompanied by severe bleeding
   D. to a limb in which there is an infected wound and there is indication of a spread of the infection

9. According to the American Red Cross, it is MOST NEARLY accurate to state that the danger of tetanus is present in _____ wounds.

   A. puncture
   B. lacerated
   C. incised
   D. all

10. All of the following men have developed a method of artificial respiration EXCEPT

    A. Schafer
    B. Neilsen
    C. Cureton
    D. Silvester

KEY (CORRECT ANSWERS)

1. D
2. A
3. B
4. C
5. B
6. A
7. D
8. D
9. D
10. C

TEST 5

DIRECTIONS: Each question or incomplete statement is followed by several suggested answers or completions. Select the one that BEST answers the question or completes the statement. *PRINT THE LETTER OF THE CORRECT ANSWER IN THE SPACE AT THE RIGHT.*

1. The recommended American Red Cross first aid care for sunburns in which the skin is blistered is the application of   1._____

    A. a burn ointment or medicated cream
    B. butter or oleomargarine
    C. a sterile, dry dressing
    D. a dressing saturated with a warm salt solution

2. The MOST serious harm from tiny foreign objects on the eye surface is   2._____

    A. their irritating effect
    B. the danger of their becoming embedded in the outer layer of the eyeball
    C. their creating an increased secretion of tears
    D. their interference with the individual's normal vision

3. All of the following are complete fractures EXCEPT a(n) _____ fracture.   3._____

    A. impacted   B. Greenstick
    C. Colles'   D. Pott's

4. The CORRECT statement in regard to the first aid care for burns is: 4._____

    A. Burns must be treated only with moist materials
    B. Greasy substances are the best medicines for all types of burns
    C. Burns must be treated only with dry materials
    D. The depth to which the body tissues are injured determines the first aid care

5. In applying a strapping to a sprained ankle, the person applying the strapping should   5._____

    A. pull the tape tight over the bony prominence of the ankle
    B. bind the toes as well as the rest of the foot
    C. have the injured foot in a position of 90 dorsi-flexion
    D. have the injured person keep the knee of the injured leg straight

6. To clean a thermometer after use, the American Red Cross advises the use of   6._____

    A. formaldehyde   B. cool water and soap
    C. peroxide   D. liquid soap in hot water

7. Hot applications should be applied   7._____

    A. in case of a sting from an insect
    B. in case of nosebleed
    C. to an ankle immediately after it is sprained
    D. none of the above cases

73

8. If a victim complains of increased pain after traction has been applied to a fractured leg, the first aider would MOST likely conclude that
   A. the traction bands are too loose
   B. the traction bands are too tight
   C. a tourniquet must be applied
   D. the simple fracture has turned into a compound fracture

9. Care of an unconscious victim, when the cause of unconsciousness is unknown, is based upon the
   A. pulse rate
   B. odor of the breath
   C. color of the face
   D. location of the accident

10. A victim of heat exhaustion will MOST likely have
    A. a moist skin
    B. a strong pulse
    C. a red face
    D. high temperature

KEY (CORRECT ANSWERS)

1. C	6. B
2. B	7. D
3. B	8. A
4. D	9. C
5. C	10. A

FIRST AID

Table of Contents

	Page
BASIC PRINCIPLES AND PRACTICES	1
Caution	1
General Rules	1
Emergency Actions	1
1. For Bleeding	1
2. For Burns	1
3. For Broken	1
4. For Shock	2
5. For Suffocation	
Artificial Respiration	3
Mouth-to-mouth (mouth-to-nose) method	3
Mouth-to-mouth technique for infants and small children	3
Other manual methods of artificial respiration	3
6. To move injured persons	3
CURRENT CHANGES IN FIRST-AID METHODS	4
Cuts	4
Bleeding from artery	4
Choking	4
Burns	5
Diving accident	5
Nosebleed	5
Poison	6
Accident	6
FIRST AID SUMMARY CHART	7

FIRST AID

Basic Principles and Practices

CAUTION
These are emergency actions only. Always call a doctor if possible. If you cannot get a doctor or trained first-aider and the injured person is in danger of losing his life, take one of the six emergency actions described in this section.

BUT, FIRST, OBSERVE THESE GENERAL RULES:
Keep the injured person lying down, with his head level with the rest of his body unless he has a head injury. In that case raise his head slightly. Cover him and keep him warm.

Don't move the injured person to determine whether emergency action is necessary. If he is NOT in danger of bleeding to death, or is NOT suffocating or has NOT been severely burned, or is NOT in shock, IT IS BETTER FOR THE UNTRAINED PERSON TO LEAVE HIM ALONE.
Do NOT give an unconscious or semiconscious person anything to drink.
Do NOT let an injured person see his wounds.
Reassure him and keep him comfortable.

EMERGENCY ACTIONS
   I.   FOR BLEEDING
         TAKE THIS EMERGENCY ACTION
            Apply pressure directly over the wound. Use a first aid dressing, clean cloth, or even the bare hand. When bleeding has been controlled, add extra layers of cloth and bandage firmly. Do NOT remove the dressing. If the wound is in an arm or leg, elevate it with pillows or substitutes. Do NOT use a tourniquet except as a last resort.

   II. FOR BURNS
         TAKE THIS EMERGENCY ACTION
            Remove clothing covering the burn unless it sticks. Cover the burned area with a clean dry dressing or several layers of cloth folded into a pad. Apply a bandage over the pad, tightly enough to keep out the air. Don't remove the pad. DON'T USE GREASE, OIL OR ANY OINTMENT EXCEPT ON A DOCTOR'S ORDER. On chemical burns, such as caused by acid or lye, wash the burn thoroughly with water before covering with a dry dressing.

   III. FOR BROKEN BONES
         TAKE THIS EMERGENCY ACTION
            Unless it is absolutely necessary to move a person with a broken bone, don't do anything except apply an ice bag to the injured area to relieve pain. If you must move him, splint the broken bone first so the broken bone ends cannot move. Use a board, thick bundle of newspapers, even a pillow. Tie the splint firmly in place above and below the break, but not tightly enough to cut off circulation. Use layers of cloth or newspapers to pad a hard splint.

Broken bones in the hand, arm, or shoulder should be supported by a sling after splinting. Use a triangular bandage or a substitute such as a scarf, towel, or torn width of sheet and tie the ends around the casualty's neck. Or place his forearm across his chest and pin his sleeve to his coat. In this way the lower sleeve will take the weight of the injured arm.

If you suspect a broken neck or back do not move the casualty except to remove him from further danger that may take his life. If you must remove the casualty, slide him gently onto a litter or a wide, rigid board. Then leave him alone until trained help arrives.

If a bone has punctured the skin, cover the wound with a first aid dressing or clean cloth and control bleeding by hand pressure.

IV. FOR SHOCK

TAKE THIS EMERGENCY ACTION

Shock may result from severe burns, broken bones, or other wounds, or from acute emotional disturbance. Usually the person going into shock becomes pale. His skin may be cold and moist. His pulse may be rapid. He may become wet with sweat. He may become unconscious.

Open your mouth wide and place it tightly over the casualty's nostrils shut or close the nostrils with your cheek. Or close the casualty's mouth and place your mouth over the nose. Blow into his mouth or nose. (Air may be blown through the casualty's teeth, even though they may be clenched.) The first blowing efforts should determine whether or not obstruction exists.

Remove your mouth, turn your head to the side, and listen for the return rush of air that indicates air-exchange. Repeat the blowing effort. For an adult, blow vigorously at the rate of 12 breaths per minute. For a child, take relatively shallow breaths appropriate for the child's size at the rate of about 20 per minute.

If you are not getting air-exchange, recheck the head and jaw position. If you still do not get air-exchange, quickly turn the casualty on his side and administer several sharp blows between the shoulder blades in the hope of dislodging foreign matter. Again sweep your fingers through the casualty's mouth to remove any foreign matter.

Those who do not wish to come in contact with the person may hold a cloth over the casualty's mouth or nose and breathe through it. The cloth does not greatly affect the exchange of air.

Mouth-To-Mouth Technique For Infants And Small Children

If foreign matter is visible in the mouth, wipe it out quickly with your fingers or a cloth wrapped around your fingers.

Place the child on his back and use the fingers of both hands to lift the lower jaw from beneath and behind, so that it juts out.

Place your mouth over the child's mouth and nose making a relatively leak-proof seal, and breathe into the child, using shallow puffs of air. The breathing rate should be about 20 per minute.

If you meet resistance in your blowing efforts, recheck the position of the jaw. If the air passages are still blocked, the child should be suspended momentarily by the ankles or inverted over one arm and given two or three sharp pats between the shoulder blades, in the hope of dislodging obstructing matter.

Other Manual Methods Of Artificial Respiration

Persons who cannot, or will not, use the mouth-to-mouth (mouth-to-nose) method of artificial respiration should use another manual method. The nature of the injury in any given case may prevent the use of one method, while favoring another. Other methods suggested for use by the American National Red Cross are THE CHEST PRESSURE-ARM LIFT METHOD (Silvester) and THE BACK PRESSURE-ARM LIFT METHOD (Holger-Nielsen).

When performing any method of artificial respiration, remember to time your efforts to coincide with the casualty's first attempt to breathe for himself.

Be sure that the air passages are clear of all obstructions, that the casualty is positioned in a manner that will keep the air passages clear, and that air is forced into the lungs as soon as possible.

If vomiting occurs, quickly turn the casualty on his side, wipe out his mouth, and reposition him.

When the casualty is revived, keep him as quiet as possible until he is breathing regularly. Loosen his clothing, cover him to keep him warm, and then treat for shock.

Whatever method of artificial respiration you use, it should be continued until the casualty begins to breathe for himself, or until there is no doubt that the person is dead.

VI. TO MOVE INJURED PERSONS

TAKE THIS EMERGENCY ACTION

Do NOT move an injured person except to prevent further injury or possible death. If you must move him, keep him lying down flat. Move him on a wide board, such as an ironing board or door, and tie him to it so he won't roll off.

If you have nothing to carry him on, get two other persons to help you carry. You must kneel together on the same side of the casualty and slide your hands under him gently. Then lift carefully, keeping his body level. Walk in step to prevent jarring, and carry him only far enough to remove from danger.

4

CURRENT CHANGES IN FIRST-AID METHODS

When an accident occurs and before medical help arrives, the victim often can be helped by someone who has knowledge of first aid. However, a person who does not know the recent developments in treatment may find that he is endangering the physical well being of the victim by using an improper method. Many of the methods once used are now obsolete. For example:

CUTS

    OLD METHOD
        Apply an antiseptic such as iodine, to a, cut to kill germs.

    CURRENT METHOD
        Wash the cut with gauze dipped in soap and water. Antiseptics can destroy living tissue around the wound and retard healing. Soap and water, however does not destroy tissue, and it provides a flushing action that washes away dirt and some bacteria.

BLEEDING FROM ARTERY

    OLD METHOD
        Apply a tourniquet to stop bleeding from a cut artery.

    CURRENT METHOD
        The best way to control any bleeding is to apply sterile compresses directly over the wound, and bandage them tightly in place. The pressure of the bandage will stem the flow of blood. Medical attention is indicated for any cut artery. The old method of using a tourniquet, say medical authorities, can be dangerous because it cuts off all circulation to the limb, which can lead to a risk of gangrene and even amputation. Also, if muscles begin to die from lack of oxygen, poisonous substances may form and get into the victim's circulation, causing "tourniquet shock."

CHOKING
    CURRENT METHOD
        Perform the Heimlich method by hugging the victim with his back against your body, placing your arms around his body. Make a fist with one hand, hold your fist with the other hand and place it under victim's diaphragm and forcefully push air up forcing food up windpipe and out of mouth. If necessary, make several separate forceful movements until successful.

    OLD METHOD
        If a person is choking, slap him on the back repeatedly in order to dislodge the obstruction.
        Do nothing for a while in order to give the person's voice box (where food usually lodges) enough time to relax. At this stage the person ordinarily coughs up the object. If nothing happens and the person stops breathing, lean him forward, then slap him on the back to dislodge the obstruction. A young child may be held upside down to help dislodge any obstruction. If the obstruction can be

reached with the fingers, it should be removed. Slapping a person immediately may cause the object to be sucked, by a sudden rush of air, into his windpipe. If the object has slipped into the windpipe, a slap may make him cough, forcing the object up against the narrower opening of the vocal cords. This can cause a blockage and asphyxiation.

BURNS

OLD METHOD

When someone is burned, apply butter or other household grease to the area.

CURRENT METHOD

Never apply grease. The sterility of household greases cannot be guaranteed and therefore there is a risk of introducing infection. In serious burns, any grease or ointment must be scraped off before treatment at a hospital, and. the patient experiences more pain. If the burn is minor (one that does not require medical attention and when the skin is not broken), sterile commercial products can be used.

Another method is to submerge the burned area in cold water (under 70 degrees) and keep adding ice to maintain the temperature. Parts that cannot be submerged should be treated with a cloth dipped in cold water. Treatment should continue until the burned parts can be kept out of the cold water without recurrence of pain. However, there is still some controversy about the use of this treatment when the burn is extensive. In a serious burn, the Red Cross recommends the application of a dry sterile dressing, bandaged securely in place to protect the burn from contamination and to prevent exposure to air.

DIVING ACCIDENT

OLD METHOD

If a person diving into the water appears to have struck his head, pull him out of the water as quickly as possible.

CURRENT METHOD

Many cases of paralysis have resulted from rough handling of a person dragged out of the water. Instead, the person should be supported in the water and kept afloat until the ambulance arrives. Quite often in this type of accident, the person's neck is fractured, and moving his head roughly is likely to cause irreparable injury to the spinal cord. If, however, it is necessary to remove a person from the water, he should be placed on something rigid so that his head will be at the same level as his body.

NOSEBLEED

OLD METHOD

Use an ice pack to stop a nosebleed.

CURRENT METHOD

Tilt the person's head all the way back so that his nose becomes the highest point of his body, and pinch his nostrils. It is important to keep the head tilted to lessen pressure. However, if the bleeding is severe, roll a piece of gauze and use it to plug his nostril, making sure that a long piece hangs out to facilitate removal. Gentle pressure can be exerted on the outside of the nostril. In severe bleeding, it is necessary to have medical attention.

POISON

OLD METHOD
Use a mixture of burned toast, tea and milk to counteract accidental swallowing of poisons.

CURRENT METHOD
Poison-control authorities say that the homemade antidote of burned toast, tea and milk is useless because the charcoal from the toast is not the kind that absorbs poisons. Call a physician immediately. Begin mouth-to-mouth resuscitation if the victim has difficulty breathing. Actually, the nature of the poison will determine the first-aid measure to use. Give water or milk. Do NOT induce vomiting if a petroleum product, such as gasoline, kerosene or turpentine has been ingested. With poisons such as an overdose of aspirin, induce vomiting by either placing a finger at the back of the victim's throat, or by giving salt water (two teaspoons to a glass) or syrup of ipecac (one ounce for adults and half an ounce for children).

ACCIDENT

OLD METHOD
Rush a person to the hospital as quickly as possible after an accident.

CURRENT METHOD
Proper carrying of an injured person is necessary in order to avoid the possibility of permanent damage. To move a person too quickly may cause spinal injury, hemorrhage or shock. Unless the person must be moved out of danger, it is BEST to apply first aid on the spot and wait until the ambulance arrives. The American Red Cross says: "The principle of first aid is to get the victim to medical attention in the best possible manner."

FIRST AID SUMMARY CHART

FOR THESE PURPOSES	USE THESE	OR THESE	SUGGESTED QUANTITY
For open wounds, scratches, and cuts. Not for burns.	1. Antiseptic Solution: Ben-zalkonium Chloride Solution, U.S.P., 1 to 1,000 parts of water.	Quaternary ammonium compounds in water. Sold under trade names as Zephiran, Phe-merol, Ceepryn, and Bactine.	3-to 6-oz. bottle.
For faintness, adult dose 1/2 teaspoon in cup of water; children 5 to 10 drops in 1/2 glass of water. As smelling salts, remove stopper, hold bottle under nose.	2. Aromatic Spirits of ammonia.		1-to 2-oz. bottle.
For shock -- dissolve 1 teaspoonful salt and 1/2 tea-spoonful baking soda in 1 quart water. Have patient drink as much as he will. Don't give to unconscious person or semiconscious person. If using substitutes dissolve six 10-gr. sodium chloride tablets and six 5-gr. sodium bicarbonate (or sodium citrate) tablets in 1 qt. water.	3. Table salt.	Sodium chloride tablets, 10 gr., 50 tablets in bottle.	1 box.
	4. Baking soda.	Sodium bicarbonate or sodium citrate tablets, 5 gr., 50 tablets in bottle.	8-to 10 oz. box.
For a sling; as a cover; for a dressing.	5. Triangular bandage, folded, 37 by 37 by 52 in., with 2 safety pins.	Muslin or other strong material. Cut to exact dimensions. Fold and wrap each bandage and 2 safety pins separately in paper.	4 bandages.

FIRST AID SUMMARY CHART (Cont'd)

FOR THESE PURPOSES	USE THESE	OR THESE	SUGGESTED QUANTITY
For open wounds or for dry dressings for burns. These are packaged sterile.	6. Two medium first aid dressings, folded, sterile with gauze enclosed cotton pads, 8 in. by 7 1/2 in. Packaged with muslin bandage and 4 safety pins.	a) Two emergency dressings 8 in. by 7 1/2 in., in glassine bags, sterilized. One roller bandage, 2 in. by 10 yds. b) Four large sanitary napkins wrapped separately and sterilized. One roller bandage, 2 in. by 10 yards.	As indicated.
For open wounds or for dry dressings for burns. These are packaged sterile.	7. Two small first aid dressings, folded, sterile with gauze enclosed cotton pads and gauze bandage, 4 in. by 7 in.	Twelve sterile gauze pads in individual packages, 3 in. by 3 in. One roller bandage, 1 in. by 10 yards.	As indicated.
For eyes irritated by dust, smoke, or fumes. Use 2 drops in each eye. Apply cold compresses every 20 minutes if possible.	8. Eye drops.	Bland eye sold by druggists under various trade names.	1/2-to 1-oz. bottle with dropper.
For splinting broken fingers or other small bones and for stirring solutions.	9. Twelve tongue blades, wooden.	Shingles, pieces of orange crate, or other light wood cut to approximately 1 1/2 in. by 6 in.	As indicated.

FIRST AID SUMMARY CHART (Cont'd)

FOR THESE PURPOSES	USE THESE	OR THESE	SUGGESTED QUANTITY
For purifying water when it cannot be boiled. (Radioactive contamination cannot be neutralized or removed by boiling or by disinfectants.)	10. Water purification tablets Iodine (trade names-- Globa line, Burso- line, Potable Aqua) Chlorine (trade name--Halazone).	Tincture of iodine or iodine solution (3 drops per quart of water). Household bleach (approx. 5% available chlorine) 3 drops per quart of water.	Tablets Bottle of 50 or 100. Liquid One Small bottle.
For bandages or dressings: Old soft towels and sheets are best. Cut in sizes necessary to cover wounds. Towels are burn dressings. Place over burns and fasten with triangular bandage or strips of sheet. Towels and sheets should be laundered, ironed and packaged in heavy paper. Relaunder every 3 months.	11. Large bath towels.		2.
	12. Small bath towels.		2.
	13. Bed Sheet.		1.
For administering stimulants and liquids.	14. Paper drinking cups.		25 to 50.
Electric lights may go out. Wrap batteries separately in moisture-proof covering. Don't keep in flashlight.	15. Flashlight.		1.
	16. Flashlight batteries.		3.
For holding bandages in place.	17. Safety pins, 1 1/2 in. lone.		12 to 15.

For cutting bandages and dressings, or for removing clothing from injured body surface.	18. Razor blades, single edge.	Sharp knife or scissors.	3.
For cleansing skin.	19. Toilet soap	Any mild soap.	1 bar.
For measuring or stirring solutions.	20. Measuring spoons.	Inexpensive plastic or metal.	1 set.
For splinting broken arms or legs.	21. Twelve splints, plastic or wooden, 1/8 to 1 1/4 in. thick, 3 1/2 in. wide by 12 to 15 in. long.	A 40-page newspaper folded to dimensions, pieces of orange crate sidings, or shingles cut to size.	As indicated.

MENTAL DISORDERS AND TREATMENT PRACTICES

This section reviews eight areas that are usually tested on examinations:

- The Characteristics of Various Psychiatric Disorders
- The Needs of Special Groups (Children, Geriatrics)
- The Influences of Environment, Society, and Family on Psychiatric Disorders
- Psychotropic Drugs (Reactions and Uses)
- The Assessment and Evaluation of Patients
- The Functions and Purposes of the Treatment Team
- The Development and Implementation of the Treatment Plan
- Methods for Handling People with Various Emotional or Psychiatric Disorders

THE CHARACTERISTICS OF VARIOUS PSYCHIATRIC DISORDERS

It is often difficult to assign labels to human behavior with any large degree of accuracy. Behavior sometimes changes rapidly, and the interpretation of what behavior a label actually represents can vary greatly from one person to the next. One can often learn a great deal more about a person by observing their behavior than by reading a diagnostic label about that person. Regardless, diagnostic labels can be helpful to members of a treatment team as a shorthand method of describing a group of behaviors one might expect from certain individuals. They are also required for many insurance forms. A diagnosis may be useful as long as one views the diagnosis as an ongoing process, and can continue to look at the patient with *new eyes*.

The Difference Between Neurosis and Psychosis

People suffering from a neurosis are usually able to manage with the concerns of daily life, although there is often some distortion in their concept of reality. Those suffering from a neurosis may feel inferior, unloved, or have a long-term feeling of fear or dread. They may have obsessions, compulsions or phobias, but they are rarely dangerous to themselves or others. They usually have some insight into their problems, and except in severe cases, don't require hospitalization. Many go through life without obtaining any help for their problems. Those who experience a psychosis, however, are out of touch with reality and live in an imaginary world. They may hear voices, feel that they are being persecuted, or experience very deep depressions. There is a very definite split between the reality of those suffering from psychoses and the reality of the world. Unlike those suffering from neuroses, those suffering from psychoses often lose track of time, person, and place, and they have little insight into the nature of their behavior. They usually require hospitalization and their behavior is sometimes injurious to other people or themselves, although they may insist that there is nothing wrong with them.

Categories of Neurosis

It is important to keep in mind that rarely will all of a patient's symptoms fall into any one category, and that symptoms may change over time from one category to another. *Anxiety Neuroses* constitute approximately 35% of all neurotic disorders. Those suffering from anxiety neuroses have a tendency to view the world as hostile and cruel, and may frequently restrict daily activities in order to feel safer in their environment. They often feel tense, worried, and anxious, but are unable to articulate exactly why they feel this way. Many anxious individuals are very uncertain of themselves in even minor stress producing situations, and they may have real difficulties in concentrating because of their high anxiety levels.

Other symptoms may include strong anxiety reactions with difficulty catching one's breath, perspiration, increased heart beat, dizziness, and feeling that they are dying. They may come to the Emergency Room of a hospital complaining of a heart attack or heart troubles. It is important to keep in mind that many elements of the anxiety reaction are seen in patients with other neurotic disorders.

Conversion Reactions or *Hysteria* involve the loss of ability to perform some physical function that the person could previously perform, which is psychogenic in origin. This reaction is an attempt by the individual to defend herself or himself from some anxiety producing situation by developing physical symptoms that have no organic or physical cause. These reactions are not common, and constitute less than five percent of neurotic disorders. The lost function is often symbolically related to a situation which has produced stress or anxiety, and is often an attempt to escape from that situation. The person may lose the ability to hear or speak, have unusual bodily sensations, or lose control of some motor function. Since there is no physical cause of dysfunction, some people assume that the pain or paralysis is not real, or that this type of person is faking. *Dissociative Reactions* also serve to protect the individual from particularly stressful situations. Amnesia, fugue, and multiple personalities are the major categories of dissociative reactions. Despite the prevalence of *amnesia* on soap operas, dissociative reactions account for less than five percent of all neurotic disorders. Amnesiacs usually forget specific information for a specified but variable period of time. The patient does not, however, forget his or her basic lifestyle or habits. In *fugue,* the person combines the amnesia with flight, and leaves the area where the stressful situation is. Usually the person is unaware of where he or she has been, or where he or she is going. There are very few cases of *multiple personalities.* In this disorder, the person shows different ways of responding to the environment. Each individual personality within the person is a complete personality system, and may dominate the person's reactions to his or her environment, depending upon the situation.

Obsessive-Compulsive Reactions involve either the inability to stop thinking about something the person does not want to think about, or the obligatory performance of a repetitive act. People experiencing these reactions often recognize they are irrational, but are unable to stop doing them. They often attempt to rearrange their environment, which they may perceive as threatening, in an attempt to impose control and structure, so they can control their environment and feel safer. Those suffering from compulsive reactions feel a strong need to perform or repeat certain behaviors, often in order to prevent something terrible from happening to them. (This might involve pre-determined ways to enter a room, brush their teeth, get into bed, begin conversations, etc.) Of course, many people may exhibit aspects of this behavior. Observing some professional baseball players before they pitch or take a pitch can certainly demonstrate this point. There is little cause for concern if the patterns are relatively temporary and help the person in some way obtain their goal. When the behaviors begin to unduly restrict a person's activities, then the situation becomes more serious. People exhibiting this behavior are often unable to make decisions effectively, are often perfectionists, have a strong need for structure, and are fairly rigid. Those who are obsessed with unwanted thoughts may have quite a variety of areas that they think about. The most common areas, however, concern religion, ethical concerns (something being absolutely right or wrong), bodily functions, and suicide.

Phobic Reactions involve a strong, persistent irrational fear of an object, condition, or place. It is believed that phobias usually involve a displacement of anxiety from the original cause to the phobic object. The phobia serves to assist the individual in avoiding the anxiety-causing situation. Some of the most common phobias include fear of crowds, being alone, darkness, thunderstorms, and high places. It is often very difficult to discover the symbolic significance of a particular phobia.

Neurotic Depressive Reactions involve an intensification of normal grief reactions. Research has indicated that those suffering from this reaction are unable to *bounce back* from upsetting or discouraging events. People who suffer from this reaction tend to have a poor self-concept, exaggerated dependency needs, a tendency to feel guilty about almost anything, and to turn those guilt feelings against themselves in a highly punitive way. The possibility of suicide should be kept in mind when working with these patients.

Categories of Psychosis

Psychoses are generally divided into two categories, *functional psychoses* and *organic psychoses*. Functional psychoses are caused by psychological stress, while organic psychoses are caused by a disorder of the brain for which physical pathology can be demonstrated. A third category, *toxic psychoses,* is sometimes used to refer to psychotic reactions caused by toxic substances such as drugs or poisons.

Schizophrenia accounts for approximately 25 percent of all first admissions to mental institutions, and is the largest single diagnostic group of psychotic patients. The *paranoid schizophrenic* shows a great deal of suspiciousness and hostility, and may be very aggressive. The *simple type schizophrenic* is shy and withdrawn, and shows interest in his or her environment. The *hebephrenic schizophrenic* often has bizarre mannerisms and may appear quite manic. He or she may laugh and giggle inappropriately, and become preoccupied with unimportant matters. The *catatonic schizophrenic* may remain motionless for days or hours, and may refuse to eat. The two phases of catatonia are the *stuporous phase* where the person is motionless and *catatonic excitement* where the person is over-active and appears manic. While the catatonic schizophrenic may alternate between these two phases, most show a preference for just one. Someone suffering from *schizoaffective schizophrenia* will have significant thought disorders and mood variations. They may initially appear to be depressed or manic, but a basic personality disorganization also exists. These are the major categories of schizophrenia you should need for the exam. Since the exam announcement states basic knowledge is required, it is very possible some of the above categories may be too specific. We have included them just in case, however.

The general symptoms of schizophrenia include an inability to deal with reality, the presence of hallucinations or delusions, inappropriate emotions, autism and various other unusual behaviors. There is often a very noticeable inability to organize thoughts. Schizophrenic reactions that occur suddenly are referred to as *acute* schizophrenic reactions, while those that develop slowly over a rather lengthy period are called *chronic* schizophrenic reactions.

Paranoid Reactions in people account for less than one percent of psychiatric admissions. Those with this behavior usually mistrust the motives of everyone, are very resentful, and often hostile. They may show signs of grandiosity or persecution. The person often believes that whatever happens is related to him or her. The major difference between paranoid patients and paranoid schizophrenics is that the paranoid patient usually has better control of his or her thought processes, and is able to make more appropriate responses to situations. They are usually more reality-oriented, and able to state their feelings more effectively.

Affective Reactions are those that represent a change in the normal affect, or mood, of a person. There are two major categories of affective disorders: *manic-depressive reactions* and *involutional psychotic reactions.* In the manic-depressive reaction, the manic and depressive states alternate. In the manic phase, the person may be extremely talkative, agitated or elated, and demonstrate a great deal of physical and verbal activity. They may also exhibit some grandiosity. In the depressive phase, the person is joyless, quiet, and inhibited. The manic reactions are often divided into three degress of severity, each category representing a more severe degree of manic reaction. *Hypomania* is the least severe, *acute mania* is the next, and *delirious mania* is the most severe state. The term *involutional psychosis is* usually related to a patient's age. For women, the involutional age is considered to be somewhere between 40 and 55, and the involutional period for men is somewhere between 50 and 65. It seems that stresses are greater for men and women during these periods, and that these stresses may trigger psychotic reactions which are generally transient. These people generally have a long history of feeling guilty and very anxious, have little diversity of activity, and few sources of satisfaction in their lives.

Selected Personality Disorders

This category includes behavior which is maladaptive, but neither psychotic nor neurotic. This group includes *antisocial reactions,* the *abuse of alchol and other drugs,* and *sexual deviations*. The *antisocial* or *sociopathic* personality type fails to develop a concern for others and uses relationships to get what he or she wants. There is little or no concern about what effect their behavior might have on others, and they seldom feel remorse or guilt. They are often likable, friendly, intelligent people. Their relationships with others tend to be superficial, however, because they lack the capacity for deep emotional responses. The sociopath is often impulsive and seeks immediate gratification of his or her wants. He or she often is unreliable, untruthful, undependable and insincere. A large number of people have sociopathic traits which, as with most other characteristics, vary in severity and number. Sociopaths are found in all professions, although many are able to control their acting out behaviors or channel them in more socially acceptable ways. They avoid acting out not because of internal values, but because they do not wish to get caught. Sociopaths usually have a low frustration tolerance, are easily bored, and continually seek excitement. The sociopath most frequently comes to treatment because he or she has been *caught* doing something or been required to seek help by an employer or family member.

Sexual Deviations occur in those who fail to develop what their society considers appropriate sexual behavior. The major sexual deviations include child molestation, rape, sadism, masochism, voyeurism, fetishism, transvestism, exhibitionism, pedophilia, and incest. As you can see, some of these behaviors are much more harmful to other people than others are.

PSYCHOTROPIC DRUGS (REACTIONS AND USES)

The two major classifications of the psychotropic drugs are the tranquilizers, which are further divided into major (or anti-psychotic) and minor (or antianxiety) groups, and the antidepressants. Other drugs used include anticonvulsants, sedatives, hypnotics, and antiparkinsons.

Tranquilizers are meant to calm disturbed patients, and free them from agitation or disturbance. Drugs designed as *antipsychotic,* or *major tranquilizers,* also help to reduce the frequency of hallucinations, delusions, thought disorders, and the type of withdrawal seen in catatonic schizophrenia. It may take several days of drug therapy before the symptoms begin to subside, but during this time the patient becomes less fearful, hostile and upset by his disturbed sensory perceptions. The *phenothiazine derivatives* are the largest group of antipsychotic drugs. All the drugs in this group have essentially the same type of action on the body, but vary according to strength and the type and severity of their side effects. These drugs include:

Thorazine	Trilafon	Taractan
Mellaril	Compazine	Navane
Stelazine	Dartal	Sordinal
Prolixin	Proketazine	Haldol
Sparine	Tindal	Loxitane
Vesprin	Repoise	Moban

Serious side effects are very important to watch for. For these drugs, the phenothiazine derivatives, there are three major types of extrapyramidal symptoms (EPS): (1) akinesia - inability to sit still, complaints of fatigue and weakness, and continuous movement of the hands, mouth, and body; (2) pseudoparkinsonism - restlessness, mask-like facial expressions, drooling, and tremors; (3) tardive dyskenesia - lack of control over voluntary movements. Symptoms may include involuntary grimacing, sucking and chewing movements, pursing of the tongue and mouth, jerking of the hands, feet and neck, and drooping head. Immediate action must be taken to combat these side effects. The administration of antiparkinson drugs usually produces a dramatic reduction in symptoms. Unless spotted and treated early, however, these can become permanent.

Other side effects may include muscle spasms, shuffling gait, skin rash, eye problems, trembling hands and fingers, fainting, wormlike tongue movements, sore throat and fever, yellowing of skin or eyes, dry mouth, constipation, excessive weight gain, edema, a drop in blood pressure when moving from a lying to standing position, decreased sexual interest, sensitivity to light and prone to sunburn and visual problems, blurred vision, drowsiness, and increased perspiration. Just about any physical symptom or behavior could be caused by a reaction to a drug.

Special Considerations: Patients receiving a high dose of a phenothiazine drug should have their blood pressure checked regularly. Long exposures of skin to sunlight should be avoided (a wide-brimmed hat and long-sleeved clothing can also help). If a patient receiving phenothiazines is lethargic and wants to sleep a great deal, the dose of the drug may be too high and need adjustment. Patients on phenothiazines should not drive or use dangerous equipment. These drugs greatly increase the effects of alcohol. In the first three to five days, a person may feel drowsy and dizzy upon standing. Antipsychotic drugs tend to mask the symptoms of diseases and dictate that patients receiving them undergo thorough physical examinations every six months.

The *Minor Tranquilizers,* or *antianxiety drugs,* reduce anxiety and muscle tension associated with it. They are useful primarily with psychoneurotic and psychosomatic disorders. When given in small doses, they are relatively safe and have few side effects. Unlike the antipsychotic drugs, some of the antianxiety drugs tend to be habit-forming. If the drug is discontinued, the person may experience severe withdrawal symptoms, such as convulsions or delirium. These drugs include:

Librium	Milpath	Frienquel
Azene	Deprol	Phobex
Tranxene	Milprem	Softran
Valium	Miltown	Atarax
Ativan	Robaxin	Vistaril
Serax	Solacen	Trancopal

Side effects may include rashes, chills, fever, nausea, headaches, poor muscle coordination, some inability to concentrate, and dizziness. Excessive amounts of these drugs may lead to coma and death; however, death is less likely with an overdose of minor tranquilizers than with an overdose of barbituates. Patients taking these should be cautioned against driving or performing tasks that require careful attention to detail and mental alertness.

Antidepressants, such as the *Tricyclic Antidepressants,* are used to elevate the patient's mood, and increase appetite and mental and physical alertness. Drugs in this group tend to take one to four weeks of use before significant changes occur in the patient's outlook. Since these drugs sometimes excite patients instead of sedating them, patients must be observed closely for reactions. These drugs include:

Elavil	Sinequan
Endep	Tofranil
Asendine	Aventyl
Morpramin	Vivactil
Adapin	Marplan
Presamine	Janimine

Common side effects include dry mouth, fatigue, weakness, nausea, increased appetite, increased perspiration, heartburn, and sensitivity to sunlight. *Serious side effects* include blurred vision, constipation, irregular heartbeat, problems urinating, headache, eye pain, fainting, hallucination, vomiting, unusually slow pulse, seizures, skin rash, sore throat and fever, and yellowing of eyes and skin.

Serious side effects include blurred vision, constipation, irregular heartbeat, problems urinating, headache, eye pain, fainting, hallucination, vomiting, unusually slow pulse, seizures, skin rash, sore throat and fever, and yellowing of eyes and skin.

Monoamineoxidose Inhibitors (MAO Inhibitors) are sometimes used for depression, but can have *very* serious side effects, and can also lead to serious hypertensive crisis. Their use must be very closely monitored. Their use with some over-the-counter drugs can be very serious. Foods containing Typtophen or Tyramine (some examples: caffeine, chocolate, herring, beans, chicken liver, cheese, beer, pickles, wine) should be avoided also. *Side effects* to watch for include severe headaches, stiff neck, nausea, vomiting, dilated pupils, and cold, clammy skin. A hypertensive crisis requires *immediate* treatment. These drugs include: Marplan, Nardil, Parnate, and Ludiomil.

In addition to the above psychotropic drugs, sedatives, hypnotics, anticonvulsants, and antiparkinsons drugs are also used. Since the exam announcement includes uses and reactions of only the psychotropic drugs, we will not review the non-psychotropic drugs. We will mention, however, the use and reactions of *Lithium Carbonate* (also known as Eskolith, Lithane,

Lithobid, and Lithonate). This drug is primarily used in the treatment of manic depressive psychoses since it is effective in decreasing excessive motor activity, talking, and unstable behavior by acting on the brain's metabolism. It also decreases swings in mood. The correct dose is close to the overdose level for this drug, so it is important to watch closely for symptoms and to report them immediately. *Common side effects* include dry mouth, metal taste, slightly increased urination, hand tremors, increased appetite, and fatigue. *Serious side effects* include greatly increased urination, nausea, vomiting, diarrhea, loss of muscle coordination, muscle cramps or weakness, irritability, confusion, slurred speech, blackout spells, and coma. These side effects require medical attention. *Special Considerations:* This drug must sometimes be taken from one to several weeks before the resident feels better. Hot weather, hot baths, and too much exercise can be dangerous, as too much perspiring can lead to an overdose. The person should drink two to three quarts of fluid a day, but should not drink large quantities of caffeine-containing beverages like coffee, tea, or colas.

www.ingramcontent.com/pod-product-compliance
Lightning Source LLC
Chambersburg PA
CBHW082213300426
44117CB00016B/2793